Tied Up in Knots

Tied Up in Knots

How Getting What We Wanted
Made Women Miserable

Andrea Tantaros

BROADSIDE BOOKS
An Imprint of HarperCollinsPublishers

HarperCollins books may be purchased for educational, business, or sales
promotional use. For information, please e-mail the Special Markets Department at SPsales@harpercollins.com.

Broadside Books™ and the Broadside logo are trademarks of HarperCollins
Publishers.

FIRST EDITION

Knot illustration by PILart/Shutterstock, Inc.

Library of Congress Cataloging-in-Publication Data has been applied for.

ISBN: 978-0-06-235186-9

16 17 18 19 20   OV/RRD   10 9 8 7 6 5 4 3 2 1

To my beloved mother, Barbara, the peaceful warrior. Dedicating the hardest thing I've ever done to the hardest thing she's ever done.

Contents

Part I

The Way We Are

Chapter 1

Tied Up in Knots

C AREFUL WHAT YOU wish for.

Women are supposed to have it together. Females aren't supposed to admit that we're tied up; not to ourselves, and especially not to each other. We're not supposed to confess that we're torn or twisted, stressed or frustrated. But honest women do. We will concede that though we've made a lot of strides, it hasn't been without a downside.

My friend Lynn recently tweeted: "All the women. In me. Are tired." Hook any woman over age thirty to a polygraph and she'll tell you that she's exhausted. She will tell you that she is under pressure. She is strained, she is conflicted, and she is trying to balance far too much in a newly minted women's world. She could be from any city or state. It doesn't matter, because her worries, her guilt, her fears are all the same.

I am one of those women. I wonder and worry about all the same things that most women do. I try to embrace being a modern female—one with money, power, and newfound privilege from the rise of feminism—with my feminine biology and my culturally traditional inclinations and values. I'm trying to balance my take-charge nature in a fast-paced, competitive workplace and field (that is still riddled with sexism), with a desire for a far more passive role in my personal relationships. No, it's not easy—but nobody ever told us it would be *this* hard.

When I was growing up, girls were told that we could do anything. We were the daughters of Betty Friedan, whose book *The Feminine Mystique* gave homemakers who wanted more out of life a chance to find their voice. Friedan advocated for more opportunity for her daughter. It was that advocacy, and the feminist movement that followed in the 1960s, '70s, and '80s, that led to my generation reaping the real fruits of feminism.

Both my parents were extremely traditional in their own way. My dad was a wonderful man, an amazing man—and a very tough father. There was some part of him that didn't want me to go to college. It wasn't that he didn't respect women; it was that he was from old-world Greece, where women focused on their Mrs. degree and baby making, and the man was the one who provided. He planned for me to work in our Allentown, Pennsylvania, restaurant. His little girl leaving home for the big city to pursue a career in politics all by herself wasn't what he had in mind. He quite literally wanted me in the kitchen making sandwiches.

My mother, on the other hand, is an evangelical Christian, traditional and old-fashioned to the core. She *still* gives me pearls to wear. She has given me solid advice on the importance of maintaining femininity, mystery, vulnerability, and softness. "Be wise as a serpent, gentle as a dove," she'd say. (Truth be told, I'm still working on that whole dove thing.) But it was my *mother* who insisted that I was going to go to college, that I was going to study in Paris, and that I was going to work in Washington, D.C.—whether my father liked it or not. This was rare for a woman who typically let her man lead. When it came to her daughters, she wanted more for us.

Needless to say, my outspoken dad didn't like it. My sister, Thea, wanted to go to D.C. after she finished college, and he forbade her. Ten years later when I was looking to do the same thing, he had the same response: no. But, ever the stubborn child, I was hell-bent on doing it anyway.

I remember packing up my Volkswagen Jetta, preparing to spend a summer interning for Pat Buchanan's presidential campaign. My father refused to speak to me. I was so upset I asked my mom if I should rethink my choice and stay home. "Absolutely not. You need to go, Andrea," she insisted. And so I did, leaving a divided household to take a big risk for a goal that was uncertain. I would never be where I am without my wise and thoughtful mom, who chose to assert her motherly mojo in this battle with my old-fashioned dad, who was pushing me toward the only life he knew. She may not look like one, in person or on paper, but my mom is a feminist icon in my eyes. She wanted exactly the same opportunity for me as parents wanted for their sons, and she wanted more for me than her father allowed her (as he opted to elevate her brothers). For that, I am forever grateful.

But for feminism, but for female power—*a female power drawing from the forgotten reality that women and men may be equal but not the same*—I would not be where I am today. If contemporary feminism believed in this and only this, we'd be a lot better off. But feminists have put forward a package deal, a bait-and-switch, and it's made millions of women miserable in the process.

Women nowadays can do just about anything men can do. We have personal and professional freedom, with the option to get married or stay single. We can freeze our eggs and wait to have kids when we're ready, and we're experiencing more success in the workplace than ever before, which means larger disposable incomes and more control over our lives than our mothers and grandmothers had. It is women who are becoming the breadwinners in many households. While the feminist movement itself has changed from what it was in the days of Gloria Steinem, the feminist message has become the cultural default. Women must dominate, and an all-male or even predominantly male organization of any kind needs to justify its existence. We won.

Feminist doctrine is not a list of wants today, it's just the way it is. It's an amorphous but understood societal norm that dictates women should be at the top, even at the expense of men. We've infiltrated everywhere, from the NFL, with our pink ribbons, to the U.S. Navy SEALs as the government is pushing women into combat roles, as some sort of gender experiment to check a box. Little do they know that women are already serving in these roles. Making it known publicly as some kind of political statement only puts the ones serving in harm's way, as our enemy doesn't realize they are there in the first place. So what is supposed to help women is actually hurting the ones currently making history. Men, for their part, have been so feminized that they dare not challenge the new culturally mandated groupthink. If they do, they are labeled sexists. It's girls who run the world; men are just unnecessary sidekicks as the lines between the sexes have increasingly been blurred. In a very real sense, we are all feminists now.

The scales started to tip in my teens. Growing up, the message in movies, music, magazines, from our teachers, professors, and parents was: You go, girl! My generation felt a deluge of motivational messages that encouraged us to capitalize on our newfound female power. When I was in high school and college I thought I could do anything. Doors opened for me. Dreams that used to seem silly were now within reach. I wasn't just *told* I was equal. I *felt* equal. I did not feel in any way insignificant or less than the guys. People went out of their way for women. My friends and I were hired at jobs and advanced fairly quickly.

While I'm truly thankful for this array of choices—far more than my mom could have ever imagined—nobody told us that there would be consequences. It almost seems like we were duped, or unintentionally misled at best. To be sure, the women who got us into these influential positions of power meant well. Granting us every option the men have is—and was—a noble and necessary goal. But I don't think they could have anticipated that advocating for women to put our careers first meant jeopardizing our fertility. Or that pushing women to be financially successful could be intimidating to men, impeding their ability to form relationships. Or that we'd still be expected to perform our household duties along with our professional ones because male culture would not adjust as quickly as we ascended.

There was a glaring observation that used to be too PC to acknowledge: women should be equal with men, but, at the same time, women *aren't* men. Equal does not mean the same. French feminist Simone de Beauvoir argued that we were "the second sex." We yearned to have rightful equality with men. But we also let our envy of the patriarchal male shape our goals. A quest for equitable treatment became a coveting of what men had: their powers, their traits, their freedoms.

Well-known feminist and author Phyllis Chesler explained to me that the movement morphed into more than just a desire to be like the guys; we wanted to be *better*. In the process, we saw a portion of the feminist movement get hijacked by man-haters. This led to an oppositional, almost adversarial relationship with men. In some respects, they were the enemy. And as often happens when you decide to make enemies, you become the thing you're seeking to correct.

Over the past half-century, females have been taught to shirk their natural wants and desires in an effort to imitate and emulate men. Any women's magazine has myriad articles giving pointers on how to be more like men in everything from sexual prowess to negotiating salaries. While much of it is necessary for our survival in a highly competitive world, some of it runs counter to our biological reality. Ironically, feminism doesn't feel very feminine.

If on the one hand we were focused, correctly, on getting respect in areas where we lacked it (such as in the office), we stopped demanding it in areas where we were used to it (such as the bedroom). This is what I call the Power Trade, and in hindsight, it was a deal with the devil. Since we had only men to emulate, since it was their power that we wanted, we foolishly began to mimic them. Instead of finding ways to channel our natural feminine qualities into our newfound roles of leadership, we abandoned our potent and precious female power, and chose to act like men. As a result, nobody is left or encouraged to behave like a lady.

While women were busy climbing, men took a backseat in modern culture. While we were ascending, we were asking, "Are men necessary?" And while we were busy reading books about the mommy track and the glass ceiling, men were following their instincts . . . which said to be supportive and listen. Men waited for women to tell them what they wanted, and we told them loud and clear. We said: We got this. You guys are released from your duties. We don't need you. Then, simultaneously, through messages sent in romantic comedies that cater to women's biological wishes and wants, we have made men essential to our self-esteem. Talk about mixed messages.

Feminists have it exactly wrong. It's not that men don't listen. It's that we told them they were superfluous, if not downright pointless. Women told men they weren't required—to pay the bill, to open the door, to help us in any way. "I can have it all" was twisted into "I can *do* it all." What a *dumb* move. Eventually if you tell someone or a certain group that they aren't needed, they'll start to believe it.

It's political conversation that's most inflammatory, most laden with emotion, most certain to cause an argument. Feminists argued that "the personal is political," and with that one simple phrase, any interaction between the genders became a cause for instant conflict. Men didn't dare argue. They just smiled and nodded, thinking that if they just went along then it would be easier for everyone. Instead, everything has now become harder for *both* genders.

Today, we women are trying to be all things to all people. We ask where all the real men have gone, but deep down we know the answer. The men, as one book put it, are on strike. Guys want to maintain the trappings of being a guy, but we aren't allowing it. The outcome is frustration, because as they say in Greece, "The bear may change its fur, but it never changes its mind." Women are afraid to admit that we screwed up, and that we need help. We can't even say that guys are useful and essential to our lives—and so we have become our own worst enemies.

While most people go along with it, I've been a keen and critical observer of cultural behavior. I've witnessed the rapid devolution of the genders for years. As a young woman I executed every directive that was pushed on me: I've manned up at work and played like a girl. I've chased men and I've let them chase me. I've cried at work and other times I've used brute force. After years of experimentation I can say what works and what doesn't. I have been a one-woman focus group on the tenets of feminism for three decades. But it wasn't until I found myself single after two back-to-back long-term relationships that I realized how different the dynamic between the sexes had become. I almost couldn't believe it. Was it just me? For the purposes of research, I pledged to stay single for at least one year. I embarked on what I like to affectionately call my Freedom Tour, a year in which I dated whomever, whenever I wanted—and some I *didn't* want.

That's when I discovered how badly men were backsliding, and how women were in full-blown panic mode. My generation, Generation X, was the cultural caboose, the last car on the train of decency, kindness, respect, and tradition. I can spot how coarsened and corroded our values have become because I knew us back when. I know what it's like to have less privilege and power as a woman but to somehow feel like you are getting more from men. I know what it's like to live in an era (despite being in my teens and early twenties) when men chased women, used

romance to woo us, and used their manly abilities to help us because we weren't ashamed to ask and they weren't scared to offer.

Now it feels like we women have more than we know what to do
with and we're dying for some backup. We're fraying at the seams.
Rather than having the courage to admit what we really want, we
seem to be stuck in our struggles, tied up in knots, and secretly
desperate to figure out ways to unbind. The America I once knew,
the one where women were climbing the ladders of success and lik-
ing it, is gone. No wonder women who came before me advised me
to enjoy the ride. Once you get to the top, the air can get thin, and
nobody gave this first and second trailblazing generation of women
a survival manual. We're virtually at the top and (aside from a few
remaining fights for rightful things like equal pay) we're pretty
much alone. We took men off the hook and insisted that they let
us take charge. In return, the days of men acting respectably—and
more important, of women demanding it—are gone, too.

Girls actress Zosia Mamet wrote in *Marie Claire* of her frustration over the complexities of dating and how we've killed romance by killing the old-time dating rituals: "Not that long ago
a guy spent the night with me. We went to breakfast the next
day. The check came. I went to the bathroom, came back. It was
still there. I thought maybe he wanted to finish his coffee. When
the waitress came to take it away, we had to address it. Seeing my
confusion, he said he didn't want to offend me by paying on 'my
side of town'—he didn't want to assert his power over mine on my
turf. So he's thinking I'd be offended, and I'm thinking, If you've
already Lewis-and-Clarked my body, maybe buy my oatmeal."

Zosia Mamet is far from what I'd call a young Republican.
She's a young woman who recognizes that something isn't right
with how things have turned out. And I knew that if liberals and
conservatives are suddenly saying the same thing, the cultural
crisis must be approaching powder-keg status. Today's societal

struggles between the sexes aren't a partisan problem. The things that we've lost, men and women alike, aren't just the concerns of those on the right. They are affecting everyone, because everyone at their core wants the same basic things. Truth be told, I am just as tied up as everyone else. But I know that unless we start to address what's causing the corrosion and come to a consensus about what's worthy of conservation, things will only get worse.

I'm not the only witness to this dramatic and depressing shift. Friends of all ages and both genders have confirmed their frustration, with study after study, article after article, and editorial after editorial filled with anecdotes that back up the bad news. Twenty-something women don't even know what being taken out on a proper date is like. Nobody picks up a telephone anymore, in a quest to avoid intimacy at all costs. We share our emotions in emojis. Rather than tell someone we feel hurt in person, we will instead agonize over the right sad face to send via text message. This is not closeness. Moral decay is running rampant, as is a desire for human decency, because we're mistreating one another as a society. We continue to dance around these issues, failing to address the root causes or feeling too scared to propose any solution, like, oh, I don't know, telling women not to publish naked selfies or have random drunk sex with just anyone. No, you cannot say those things.

The reality that we are a culture in crisis can no longer be ignored. Girls and boys, it's time we stop feeling miserable and muster the will—and the courage—to have this discussion. It takes a conservative to see that our culture has coarsened, that our genders are in crisis, and that our relationships are being ruined. And it will take a conservative to help us recognize the things most important to all of us that are worth conserving. It's not too late to save the things we value and have the relationships we want. We can get them back if we can break free of the bad habits of our time—and finally start to untie the knots.

Chapter 2

Twisted Sisters

F EMINISM IS COMPLICATED. Anytime estrogen is involved, there is bound to be drama. I met Mika Brzezinski when I used to appear on MSNBC, before Fox News put a ring on it. In addition to Mika's regular duties as cohost of *Morning Joe*, she sometimes filled in as a daytime anchor when I was a guest. I always admired her cool, calm nature, and her striking looks. There are very few women who look as good at age fifty as they did at age thirty—and Mika is one of them.

After Fox hired me full-time in 2011 I stopped appearing on other channels and rarely came into contact with the competition. Later that year, my path with Mika crossed again at a charity event at Milly, a clothing store on the Upper East Side. She saw me approach her out of the corner of her eye but continued to stand there and talk to her friend. I patiently waited for her to end her conversation and then gave her a smile. The look she gave me in return was less than thrilled. I guess Mika Brzezinski wears her emotions on her face. Well, I could certainly relate to that.

"Hi, Mika."

"Hello . . . ?"

"I'm Andrea Tantaros. You used to interview me on MSNBC from time to time. I'm on *The Five* now."

She furrowed her brow as if trying to search for recognition. It was like she'd forgotten where she'd left her keys. "Hmm."

After a while it became awkward. "Anyway, nice to see you."

"Wait, what's your name?"

"Andrea Tantaros."

"And *what* show are you on?"

"*The Five.*"

She kept squinting, her head cocked. *Were they in the glove compartment? Maybe they fell under the seat?* "And where did you say you worked again?" she said, never losing her squint.

At the time, *The Five* was the second-highest-rated show in all of cable. Mika was either A) embarrassingly uninformed about what was happening in her industry, or B) simply choosing to act like the nastiest woman on the Upper East Side—and that's no mean feat. "*The Five,*" I repeated. "On Fox News."

"Ohhhh . . ." she said, nodding. "You work at Fox because you're *preeeettty.*"

Yep, Mika was B. The condescension was gross and terribly obvious. It was also really disappointing from someone so successful, someone whom I had admired. "No," I told her, "I work at Fox because I'm smart." We stood there for a second before we both kind of turned away.

Unlike Mika, I didn't have dad's coattails to ride. My father was an immigrant from Greece, with zero connections to help me get where I am today. But what he *did* give me was a sense for being polite to people and a mandate to not be ungracious—especially when dealing with professional colleagues.

Mika had written about struggling with eating disorders in her book *Obsessed.* Was that why she felt the need to cut down people like me? Was it self-doubt and malicious insecurity? Curious, I read her other book, *Knowing Your Worth.* In it, Mika interviewed a bunch of notable powerhouses who have "navigated the inevitable roadblocks that are unique to women" about the "pitfalls they face." Little does the reader know that the author herself exemplified one of those potential pitfalls—and that she was hardly unique in this regard.

There's an Internet meme called Actual Advice Mallard, which features a duck dispensing useful truths: "Reread books and rewatch movies at different times in your life. The stories don't change, but your perspective does." "Buy yourself a Yelp T-shirt. You will receive excellent customer service anywhere you go." My favorite: "Men, don't try to understand women. Women understand women and they hate each other."

While *all* women don't hate each other, competition among females for money, men, and status is fiercer than ever. There are many articles about misogyny in the workplace and the boys' clubs that exist in different industries. But nowadays it's not only the guys who are responsible for keeping us down. As women become increasingly successful, we're turning our female power against each other.

I sometimes joke that my years in a sorority gave me a black belt in understanding bad female behavior (not to imply that maliciously insecure, vindictive female behavior is limited to sororities—if only). But even the cattiness of the sorority house didn't prepare me for how oppositional women would be at virtually every stage in my career. The worst part is knowing that it doesn't have to be that way. There are many women who—like men—realize how important cultivating relationships is in any industry. The really smart ones understand that having other bright women on set only helps a given show and network. When I worked in Washington, D.C., I helped a friend of a friend named Marny Cavanaugh get a job at Fox News. Years later, she returned the favor by giving me my first on-air opportunity, on Martha MacCallum's old show *The Live Desk*. Being a connector pays off for everyone involved, and I will be forever grateful to Martha.

Not every woman is like Martha MacCallum. For every Martha, there's a rival newswoman who likes to refer to Fox News Channel as "legs and lashes." We may wear more eyelashes at Fox than at other networks, but we are also number one, so there is bound to be some professional jealousy.

Attorney Miriam González Durántez often speaks out against females who stand in the way of their own. "Women have spent years talking about the glass ceiling. But I think it's very important we don't create a glass floor, so that the women who get there throw the ladder away and say 'nobody else.'" Because of the women who paved the way before us, contemporary career women don't have to go to jail or die for our rights. That's something I feel very grateful for. But I also agree with Durántez's point. As the glass ceiling has become chipped away from every angle, it's become replaced by a glass floor—one built by and against other women. Just look at how Madeleine Albright treated women during the 2016 presidential election, when she was stumping for one-woman glass floor Hillary Clinton. "There's a special place in hell for women who don't help other women," she lectured. What about women who bully other women? Do they, like Clinton and Albright, get reserved seating? On the heels of Albright's comments, feminist icon Gloria Steinem then insulted women for supporting Hillary's opponent. "Young women back Bernie because 'the boys are with Bernie.'" And to think, all this time I thought women were told we had a right to choose. I guess not when it comes to our political choices. What's worse is that the comments of these women weren't empowering, they were insulting. We're horny and we're going to hell if we don't see things your way. So much for sisterhood.

The arenas in which female power has proven harmful have

expanded as our power bases have grown. When women were in the home, female fighting was relegated to PTA meetings, workout classes, or in social settings (usually over men). But now there's more hostility directed by females at other females, *especially* in professional settings.

Today's feminists heap much of the blame for keeping women down on men. But in 2014, Gallup released a report showing that Americans preferred having a male boss to a female one. *Women* chose a male boss over a female one by a 13-point margin. In my experience, men in positions of power tend to be less inclined to act as roadblocks. Even the *Wall Street Journal* noted that the "tyranny of the Queen Bee" is on the rise, and it stings.

The term is quite apt. The *Journal* reporter Peggy Drexler described such a tyrant as "[t]he female boss who not only has zero interest in fostering the careers of women who aim to follow in her footsteps, but who might even actively attempt to cut them off at the pass. Far from nurturing the growth of younger female talent, they push aside possible competitors by chipping away at their self-confidence or undermining their professional standing. . . . Women are finding their professional lives dominated by high school 'mean girls' all grown up: women with something to prove and a precarious sense of security."

This eating-your-own carnage is *everywhere*. It's in Hollywood, in media, in finance, in the so-nice world of nonprofits. Chris Rock jokes, "Every woman thinks there's a woman at work who is trying to destroy her," even if it's a Macy's and she works in the gift-wrapping department. My first boss out of college didn't just have the stereotypical high maintenance, alpha-female attitude; it was straight-up bullying. She'd criticize trivial things like my manicure: "That's an *interesting* choice. Looks like something my teenage daughter would pick out." (*Red?*) Her digs at my appearance were *constant*. "Somebody looks tired in this meeting. Late night?" In fact, the only thing I was tired of were her constant personal jabs, which were entirely unrelated to my performance.

She ran hot and cold, and I was held victim to her violent mood swings. One minute she'd be drawing me in with compliments or venting about personal details of her nasty divorce as if we were old friends. The next minute she'd be snapping at me, berating me in front of other staff, or slamming the door in my face. It was awful.

As the boss, clients often sent her gifts. Anything fattening she would pass on to me, trying to get me to eat candy because I was supposedly "too thin" and needed to "put some meat on my bones." I felt like Gretel! I was hardly emaciated. She was just trying to think of ways to make me look—and feel—as insecure and miserable as she was. I find it hard to believe that any male boss would act this way. Men simply aren't that creative in their cruelty.

These mean-girl antics are very tough to combat, and this was especially the case for me since I was so green. To whom could I complain? Her digs weren't overtly confrontational and were often hidden in softer speak. Men who were above my boss didn't pick up on the passive-aggressive nature of her prodding, or how she was always gossiping about me to others in the company. It often takes a lot for men to even realize that their own wives are upset. How could they be expected to zero in on my boss's subtle undermining? How could I even explain it myself? "She tells me I should eat more"? All she'd do was claim that she was offering me candy as a nice gesture, and that I was being too sensitive.

The problem with this sort of persistent assault is that the emotional impact is impossible to explain accurately. Each little dig is so innocuous in and of itself that it only becomes a problem once it's a pattern—and patterns generally need to be experienced to be understood. It's one thing to be told that it sucks to live in a city where it rains every day for months, and it's another thing to actually spend time there.

One of the greatest strengths we have as women is our ability to understand emotions and nonverbal cues. Men tend to be oblivious to such things, even when they themselves are the culprits. This is perhaps the classic miscommunication between the sexes, where the curt, all-business guy horribly upsets the perhaps overly sensitive female. Both parties are acting "normally," but neither is happy or productive. Her being upset for "no reason" only confuses and irritates him, which encourages him to be more curt, and so on.

Part of the power trade was the assumption of male characteristics by women—and this is a trade that suits the queen bees perfectly. Let's take the archetypical male villain: the abusive husband or boyfriend. Feminists fought for decades to demonstrate to America that abuse is far, far more common than people were willing to admit. They educated the public to understand that psychological abuse is more frequently the pattern than physical abuse and that it is often more dangerous because it is harder to identify and demonstrate. Feminists had to show that just because a woman doesn't have a black eye and bruises doesn't mean she's not suffering real harm and damage.

I freely admit that this was an enormously important contribution that feminists made to our culture. Yes, I do part company with the contemporary definition of abuse, which sometimes can mean "not doing what a feminist wants in a relationship" or "encouraging a woman to make the compromises that every partnership demands." But the broader point is true and remains.

Now imagine this archetypical husband and how he deals with his wife. Let's take a common scenario: the abusive assault on the woman's intelligence. One comment is not going to be

abuse. Every person on earth has had a brainfart. We've all gotten one really obvious question wrong playing trivia, or completely forgot what we needed to buy at the store, or had some
hilariously bad typo. These types of incidents are so funny and
not indicative of being dumb that we frequently are the first to
share them with our friends. One can easily imagine President
Obama chuckling about the time he said that there were fifty-
seven states.

Though one comment about someone's intelligence can be innocuous or even humorous, there's no precise point where it becomes an issue and then abuse. It's not quantifiable. Yet anyone
can see that if a husband brought up the fact that his wife had a
brainfart *every single day* then that would become abusive before
long. His point would be that this wasn't some one-off incident
but proof that she was dumb. It works the other way as well. A
wife who daily made comments on her husband's intelligence
would eventually sound ironic and then sarcastic. I'm sure that
after a few months even Albert Einstein would have to question
why his wife, Elsa, kept bringing up his mind, unless there was
some deeper, less positive subtext.

If people can understand how this works in a relationship,
they should be able to understand how this works in the office.
The passive-aggressive (or sometimes just plain aggressive) process is exactly the same. A boss commenting on a subordinate's
figure every day is not going to make her feel comfortable. She
will start to feel that something must be wrong with her body—
and will stress over being unable to determine exactly what that
something her boss is referring to is. That's when the female
mind fills in the blank with its own insecurities, and the sense of
humiliation is complete.

Feminists are not philosophically equipped to address this. They are so enamored with the idea of powerful women and so protective of them that they can't acknowledge that sometimes these powerful women are just as horrible as powerful men—if not more so. Then, when these women are attacked, the feminist cry is that the accuser is simply scared of powerful women. That's an easy claim to make against a guy, but I think it might be tough to prove that I personally am threatened by powerful women. The only powerful woman I'm scared of is my mom, and that's only because she has some really embarrassing pictures of me as a teen lying around.

I wish I had some sort of magic wand to advise how to deal with these types of women. I have no problem admitting it's a tough situation without a simple solution. My preferred strategy is to address such behavior as professionally as possible right when it happens. I try to calmly recount what just happened so that I could go on record to show the abusive boss that her behavior was wrong and I *know* it's wrong, and that I won't be her victim. It's useful to have a witness nearby so the queen bee can't spin the story her way, but the better ones are too crafty to be caught in front of a third party. If it gets worse? *Run.* That's what I did, and not a minute too soon. I take comfort in this: when evil people set a trap for the good, they always end up falling into it themselves. You really do reap what you sow.

It felt great when I eventually quit that job. It was scary not having another position lined up, but I would rather have waited tables than work another day for someone so emotionally destructive. I had managed to stick it out for a time far longer than I should have, fearing that having a brief stint on my resume would make it look like I'd been fired. It took another female—a mentor—to tell me what I should have done in that situation. "All a potential employer needs to hear," she told me, "is that it 'wasn't a healthy work environment.' Believe me, they'll get the message loud and clear."

I was lucky, since unlike so many others my story had a happy ending. When I was working on Capitol Hill years later, I saw my former boss's name on the guest list for a meeting that I was leading. She had wanted to come pitch a business deal to my current boss, another very powerful woman. I could have gotten her disinvited from the meeting. Instead, I just watched her face melt when she saw me. Notoriously unprepared, she seemed even more uncomfortable that day. Needless to say, her firm didn't secure the project. I didn't need to sabotage her; she did that all by herself. *The queen bees always forget that the biggest bitch out there is karma.*

That's just one way that women tie other women up in knots. Other women choose to be bullies *out of principle*. They feel that because they've had to fight so hard to rise through the ranks, no one should have it easy. They believe that everyone needs to earn it the same way that they did, and live by an every-woman-for-herself mentality.

These types typically have seen success in traditionally male-dominated fields and don't respect any female in the workplace until she's sufficiently paid her dues. A movement rooted in a history of being mistreated and abused is now often the vehicle for doing the abusing. My first boss explicitly identified as a feminist. She would recount stories of being the only woman in the room and having to learn to fit in with the boys. She constantly boasted that she was one of the few female executives in the company. To her, this was a source of great pride—as well it should have been! It becomes a problem when women who saw themselves as victims of inequality and mistreatment use their newfound power not to nurture their own but to perpetuate sexism against them.

I've seen this phenomenon a lot in politics. I recall asking a whip-smart woman what it was like to work for Senator Dianne Feinstein on the Judiciary Committee. "She's tough," the woman said. "Really tough."

Tough could be good or it could be a euphemism, as I've had to learn for myself. "But is she mean?" I pressed.

"No, she's fair. And she's not a bitch. She's worked really hard to bust through that glass ceiling and feels that, because of that struggle, she's not going to go out of her way to make it easy for other women."

It's not an evil perspective. It makes emotional sense. But that doesn't make it any easier for the young woman on the receiving end, especially from someone whom she would otherwise regard as a true role model. This cold-bloodedness is hardly limited to the political left. I saw the same thing with female Republicans for whom I worked throughout the years. They typically liked me because they knew I was producing for them and was fiercely loyal—but all the same, they were still harder on me than on the men.

It can be quite difficult for women to treat female colleagues as colleagues, as opposed to rivals in some weird high school sense. One female boss was so personally hurt when she found out that I'd taken another, better-paying, more challenging job that she wouldn't even speak to me on my last day in the office. This was after years of working by her side.

After not seeing her for almost a decade I ran into her when a mutual friend gave us a ride to an event. I had just started working at Fox and was over the moon to get reacquainted, but she played it cool and tried to ignore me. It was heartbreaking. Yet when she later came around and needed a favor, I gladly helped her out. I didn't want to be vindictive despite how she had made me feel. I had become a better person because of working with her. She had been kind and inspiring to me at some point, and I didn't want to pretend like that had never happened—even if *she* did. I knew her animosity wasn't personal. It wasn't me so much as what I represented.

I couldn't completely resent her. Her hard work and sacrifice was giving me opportunities that she never had. She sowed the crop but then had to stand by and watch me and my generation reap the harvest. There I was, in my twenties, with a promising career ahead of me—minus the barriers that she and her peers had broken down. She, on the other hand, had to try to balance the crushing pressures of a demanding career in the public eye with real friends being few and far between. It's lonely being a pioneer. There's almost no one alongside you, by definition. It's especially lonely being a female pioneer. When we climb the ladder of success, we do it in heels.

Of course, not all strong women stick that four-inch heel in the eye of our adversaries down the professional ladder, or act rougher on members of their own gender. Many women take an opposite approach, fostering the progress of other females, giving advice or making introductions for like-minded or compatible colleagues. I know quite a few highly accomplished women in positions of power who have been and still are trusted mentors. These women were secure enough to believe in me, rather than belittle me behind my back.

But it's not just supervisors or bosses who can be abusive. There's also the coworker who tries to be your work buddy in order to backstab and use your office friendship to undermine you. Like Jennifer Jason Leigh's character in *Single White Female*, they wake up in the morning thinking of new ways to destroy their targets. They're so unsure of their own capabilities that they see every female rising through the ranks as a foe, and they some-times cozy up to their supposed competitors with a keep-your-enemies-closer mentality.

Instead of spending time honing their own skills and worry-ing about their own position, they scheme and obsess. They use their phony camaraderie like currency with superiors and other coworkers, spreading gossip about their targets under the guise of concern: "I don't know if Andrea can handle the assignment you gave her. She's been really emotional lately. I fear she's not stable." I learned that one frenemy of mine said those exact words to our boss. And since the boss perceived us to be close—we *were* always chatting—he of course believed her.

These types watch their target's every move, from what she wears to who she dates. If they can't find things to criticize they'll just make something up: "Have you been able to get a hold of her? She hasn't responded to my emails. I think she might have a drinking problem." There is no point in agitating women like this, let alone going to war with them. This is a case where I (of all people) advocate against confrontation and aggression lest it be perceived as a stereotypical catfight. The key is to keep them at arm's length, if not further. No one comes out of a fight with a skunk without smelling bad. Your time is always better spent worrying about yourself and working harder than they do, so you become undeniable and unquestioned in your abilities. "Cream rises," Megyn Kelly once told me. "The spoiled stuff gets thrown out."

Many people, especially early feminists, hoped that cama-raderie among women would flourish in an environment that celebrated and facilitated female advancement. They hoped that more power in the workplace would lead to more mentoring, more unity, and the fostering of female growth and bonding. But more women working has made room for more malice. A

2011 survey of one thousand working women by the American Management Association found that 95 percent of respondents believed they were undermined by another female at some point in their careers. That's almost universal.

Women in the workplace need to wake up. Though we've accomplished much, much should still be expected. We need to be more careful and cognizant in how we treat our gender. While I'm not advocating that all women become part of some sisterhood (it's just not in everyone's nature and that's fine), it's important that we don't make deliberate moves to subvert it. Men and women can argue about many things, but one thing is certain: *women never forget a slight.* Crossing a fellow female will always have negative repercussions down the road. Besides, it's wasted energy. Eagles don't fly with pigeons.

Smart, secure women elevate other women. It's beneficial to be superb at networking with a band of loyal Louboutin-clad foot soldiers. The more you help people, the more they're inclined to help you. Kindness to others gets paid back in loyalty. No one can be in every cubicle, but having loyal colleagues means you *can* have eyes and ears everywhere. They can identify those who seek to undercut you. Like the Beach Boys song goes, "You need a mess of help to stand alone."

I always advise people, especially women, to be connectors. The same talents that made women matchmakers over the centuries work wonders in the office. While it can sometimes feel like no good deed goes unpunished, being the glue, putting people in touch with those who can help them, always gets paid back tenfold. It goes both ways, too. I always do my best to reward loyalty. It's good ethics and it's good strategy. Nothing feels as good as returning the favor for someone who stuck her neck out on your behalf. Power—the kind that women have pursued for decades—is pointless when it's not also used to help others.

Chapter 3

Wound Too Tight

ANDREA, YOU'RE REALLY smart and really . . . *tough*."
It was a television exec talking, and I wasn't sure if he
was actually complimenting me or saying it as a slight (or maybe
both). You never really know how to take these things as a female. I decided to accept it as praise. "Thank you!" I said with a
grin. I'm proud when anyone says I'm tough, because—like it or
not—that's who I authentically am. Not being tough can imply
weakness, and like most career women I'm much less comfortable with that label.

When I was a fairly rebellious teen, my father used to say,
"Caution." "You're gonna get yourself in trouble," he would warn
in his thick Greek accent. "You don't listen." He typically said it
with exasperation, tired of arguing with me over things like an
earlier curfew and how boy crazy I was. In my defense, my father
was very strict. When I fought with him it was for benign things
like being allowed to go to school dances or to sleep over at a
friend's house. I never drank in high school, I got good grades,
and was always working at our restaurant—which kept me out
of trouble.

Even though I was an angel(ish) by most modern-day standards, my dad was raised in old-world Greece. He just didn't

want to see me make a mistake that I would regret. He had sacrificed too much to come to this country, and viewed his rules as a way to protect me. "You can take your father out of Greece but you can't take the Greece out of your father," my mom would say when I asked her to intervene. Surely he would have preferred it if I'd been born with my sister Thea's quieter, more obedient demeanor.

As I got older my dad realized that I wasn't getting in as much trouble as he thought I would. He saw that he'd probably been too harsh with me and we grew much closer. Before he passed away from cancer in December 2009, he came to view my thick skin as I did and still do: a badge of honor. He was relieved that I was so strong and could handle myself, especially since I was living on my own in New York City and just beginning my TV career.

After his funeral, his best friend Jimmy told me how they'd once discussed their respective daughters and marriage. Jimmy's daughter had been going through a terrible separation, but he wanted me to know that my father hadn't been worried about me screwing things up in the same way. "Andrea," he had said, "she's not gonna make a mistake. She's smart and strong, like me."

This confession almost brought me to tears. Not only was it a memory of my dad that I hadn't heard, but it validated nearly three decades of tenacity. It reminded me of all the arguments that we used to have at home and in the restaurant kitchen in front of the staff. It could have been over anything, like how many tables my father was loading up in my section at one time or that I wasn't keeping the other waitresses in line. That same combative aspect of my personality that used to make him crazy had finally brought him some peace and comfort.

If there is a prediction I wanted him to be right about, it's that one (and he was). Plus, I know my dad was right in a

broader sense. I *am* a lot like him and the mother who raised
him: very, very strong. I don't think of myself as tough in a bad
way. I'm proud of my bluntness and prefer to regard it as having a very low tolerance for BS. In television, you need to have
a thick skin and be strong in order to survive, let alone thrive.
The business is so rough-and-tumble that the faint of heart do
not last. The minute you stop being strong is the minute you
stop excelling.

Yet professional potency can also have its downsides. If you're
a tough cookie, both men and women can respect you or sometimes fear you. With the grit comes the title of "bitch" or "mean
girl." Those are hard terms to shake, even though they often
aren't accurate. I've been called both but am neither. I've worked
for women who are incredibly effective in male-dominated fields
like politics, and they get the same rap. With women increasingly in positions that men used to hold, we find ourselves in
the same constant competition that the men used to have. This
is a large part of the power trade that feminists made when they
pushed for equal rights. Now that women have those rights, we
also have the power that comes with them—and much like the
guys did, we're fighting to keep it.

For decades, we've been encouraged by feminists to fight
for whatever it is that we want. We fought to get the vote. We
fought for the right to legally hold property, and for the right to
be recognized as equal but different individuals with needs and
desires unlike those of men. These days it feels like women have
to fight for everything. We fight to balance work and career. We
fight for a promotion, we fight to save our marriages and relationships, and we fight to be treated equally in the workplace. Fight,
fight, fight! But it's *how* we fight that gets us ahead and earns us
respect.

While we have friendly and respectful disagreements on *Out-*

numbered, I started my television career battling with Democrats. The segments often got pretty heated. The formula was me versus an older liberal (typically Bob Beckel) or some woman from the opposite side of the aisle (catfight!). Because I was only in my twenties at the time, I felt that I needed to be tough in order to be taken seriously. If I was demure then I wouldn't seem legitimate and my opponents would eat me for lunch. There could only be one winner, after all.

This increasing aggression came back to bite me. Typically we would crack jokes after wrapping *America's Newsroom*, but one morning Bob just stormed off the set after a debate. I had never seen him so upset. "Are you mad at me?" I asked him later.

"You called me a liar on national television," he fumed. "That hurt my credibility and it hurt me as your friend."

I was stunned. Bob had said a lot of very out-of-line comments to me over the years. Some were sexist, some were just plain stupid and offensive, but we had worked through them with him offering up a sincere apology. This was the first time that he had ever called *me* out. "I'm sorry, Bob. I truly am. I'll never do it again."

It was the first time I realized that my take-no-prisoners approach was damaging my professional relationships. This wasn't just any relationship, either. If I was going to continue on-air with Bob or *any* sparring partner, I had to be respectful and get my power in check—*especially* because I was a young woman. I couldn't risk being seen as snotty, particularly with someone I cared for as deeply as I did Bob. Going forward I never did it with him again and always chose my words carefully when we argued. This was an especially useful lesson to learn before being cast on not one, but two ensemble shows.

Women have it harder than the men do. I'm not saying that to be a victim, I'm saying that to be a truth teller. When I was starting out in my career I believed that wasn't the case. I graduated from college thinking I could do anything. One benefit of liberal academia is that women are elevated (often at the expense of men). When I started working in Washington, D.C., I felt that I had total equality. But as I got older and more successful, I saw that women are still treated differently. Women who say they've never been treated a certain way because of their gender are simply lying or delusional. Sexism is still running rampant, though it's not as simple as oppression of females anymore.

People expect men to be ambitious, and they're often rewarded for it. But when a woman is determined and strong-willed, she can get a reputation and be *punished* for it. I've had bosses who liked my tenacity and those who despised it. On political campaigns I've worked for men who appreciated it when I attacked reporters for asking unfair questions. Once I literally went after— yes, physically chased—a reporter who was doing live shots on then–Massachusetts governor William Weld's lawn after he told me he wouldn't respect the family's privacy. The governor appreciated my fire, fueled by my loyalty to him. If I had to knock on doors, I didn't hesitate. On the other hand, my potency hasn't always played out so well, especially with alpha males who tend to resent or feel threatened by it.

So which is the best choice for women like myself? There isn't one single guideline that captures exactly how women should best use their female power in the workplace. That's the bad news. The good news is that we do have options. We can choose to act however we'd like depending on what result we want. But we have to be prepared to deal with the consequences, just as men do.

As I've matured I've started to see that power applied properly can be effective. Once, seconds before we were going live on the set of *Outnumbered*, an argument broke out between two of the fill-in cohosts. I wasn't about to tolerate tension on the show and risk having bad chemistry on-air. I immediately shut it down by telling everyone in a strong but respectful tone to knock it off.

Even though I did the right thing, the best thing for the show, it could have been perceived as an overreaction. Truthfully, I didn't care. I had to be the adult in the room and did what was best for the program and for the network. If the show went off the rails that day it would have been my head on the chopping block just as much as anyone's. Yet when I've seen men do similar things, I doubt there's ever been any whispering about them. They were being leaders, whereas I was being pissed-off.

Women have always been powerful creatures. It's only now that we're so omnipresent in the workplace that we have to learn to try to manage our potency. It's also taken some getting used to by the guys. Many men struggle in trying to adapt to females using their professional power. For decades men have been taught not to lose to a girl. A workplace dispute against a smarter or more prepared female can be tough for many men to take. If a woman is promoted over a man or is proven correct in a disagreement it can come off as downright emasculating for a guy. To discuss these emotions isn't to justify them, of course. But denying that these things happen doesn't help either gender move forward.

Despite this progress, male culture doesn't really focus on helping guys grapple with this new gender panorama. *Esquire* will tell a guy what man purse to buy, but it hardly ever has in-depth pieces on working with a macho female superior. *GQ* will give tips on how to pick up a hot woman at a bar, but never give tips on how to date a strong one. As more men raise daughters in an environment filled with female power, the norms are shifting in a positive way.

In 2015 Facebook exec and author of the cult sensation *Lean*

In Sheryl Sandberg coauthored an article for *Esquire* with her late husband, Dave Goldberg. The two tried to help men adjust their outlook toward this new trend of successful women. Their pointers could not have been more spot-on. Men shouldn't underestimate females, they said. "I've played in the World Series of Poker," Goldberg recalled, "and female pros do better on average because people assume they are worse than they are." He also advised men to help with the housework because it will get them more sex, and to be more open to women at the workplace because most men have sisters and daughters. "How would you want them to be treated?" he asked.

What cracked me up is that the pointers about complimenting powerful women, while better than nothing, are only given to benefit the man. There is no case made to compliment a strong, successful woman because it's the right thing to do. Instead, it's because the guy will get more action, won't look dumb underestimating girls, and has got a sister and basically karma's a bitch. A more honest assessment would be "Since you can't beat them, join them. You're equals!" But that may be a far too inconvenient and annoying truth.

As the saying goes, "If you want to test a person's character, don't give him money—give him power." Just as men have been tested throughout the centuries on how they've handled power, now women are being tested with newfound power as well. Finding that pitch-perfect balance—knowing when and how to assert one's strength—is the greatest challenge for anyone. Women often have an urge to play the victim, but I caution colleagues against it. If I feel like I'm being treated in a way that a man wouldn't, I point it out and move on. Sometimes I win, other times I don't. But I find the best route is to have the courage to call it out without losing momentum. Arguing that we should be treated differently because of our gender runs counter to everything that we fought for. Either we play by the same rules or we don't—even if others aren't willing.

I once did an interview and was asked a personal question by a pervert posing as a journalist: "How does it make you feel that so many people talk about your breasts online?"

Young Andrea would have reached across the couch and strangled him. Instead I simply asked if he would ask a male journalist the same question about his penis.

He looked stunned. I paused, and with a steely glare looked him right in the eyes.

"We're done here. This interview is over." I stood up and walked out. Degrading him personally wouldn't have made the situation better. Just because he was rude and boorish didn't mean I had to return the disrespect. It would have simply made *me* look bad and ruined the story. Calmly shutting it down was power. Controlling emotion took even more strength but there it was: a skill and lesson in discipline that took me years to hone, one that most men won't ever learn. My mom always said, "the hardest thing to control is the tongue."

I sympathize with women who aren't as naturally tough as I am. People aren't expecting such women to assert themselves—and people rarely adjust well to surprises about their perceptions of others. It's harder for the less potent workplace female to step up and flex her muscles than for the feisty one who is only acting as her coworkers expect her to. Sure, the sheepish one's message can seem worthwhile. If the quiet girl raises her voice, then maybe we're missing something. More likely, however, she'll be pegged as having overreacted. "Did you hear how Jackie lost it out of nowhere? It's the quiet ones you have to watch out for!" As women we often can't win. Female power in the workplace is a double-edged stiletto.

One of the greatest hurdles that women face today is learning to turn that fighting spirit off in our love life, getting out of butt-kicking mode after we leave the boardroom and enter the bedroom. Shoes are easy to take off after work; attitudes, not so much. In my twenties my spitfire personality served me well in politics and on campaigns. If doors weren't always easy to open, I had no qualms about kicking down a few or prying open a window. In my personal life, however, it was harder to turn off Xena warrior, even though I longed for the type of intimacy with my partner that opened the door for vulnerability. That masculine version of power proved to be a romantic turnoff to many men. Men don't respond well to confrontation with other men. Why would we expect them to be drawn to it in women?

In my experience I've found that most men simply aren't sure how to handle a potent woman. Many a female friend has mused that she thinks her powerful nature intimidates her boyfriend. It doesn't help that magazines and romantic comedies paint successful women as heroes at work but terrifying monsters in dating and marriage. I have also found that women who emasculate their men don't do it out of strength but out of weakness. It stems from an unhappiness or insecurity with themselves or their relationship.

There are the few men who really appreciate it. I'm lucky I found one who not only values my strength but can also match my fire. "I love how strong you are," he once told me. "It's really hot." I have a deep love and respect for such men, but they're quite rare. Many of these types probably wouldn't appreciate my strength if I wielded it against *them*. But I had to learn that lesson the hard way.

Sam and I had been dating for less than a year. Since it was a long-distance relationship, that made our weekends together all the more precious. At the same time I'd recently started appearing on Fox News to talk about the 2008 presidential election, in addition to working full time as vice president of a public affairs firm. And since even *that* wasn't enough for me, I was also a New York *Daily News* columnist. I was stressed out and spread very thin workwise.

One Friday night Sam and I had plans to go out to dinner. I was late as usual, this time due to appearing on *Hannity & Colmes*. Rather than ruin our Friday night together, Sam waited until the following morning to reveal that he had been upset. "You're always late," he told me.

"This is my career," I said. "You know how important it is that I accept whenever they offer me an appearance."

"I understand that, and I support that. But all I want you to do is to acknowledge your lateness and say that you're sorry."

"I'm *not* sorry. I had to do this."

It turned into a massive fight that went on for more than twenty minutes. Ever the tireless debater, I made the entire argument about how Sam needed to be more flexible. The truth was, I was putting my career first and he was not being understanding, but I was being defensive and argumentative. Sam was ten years older than me and had more relationship experience. "I'm not Bob Beckel," he finally said.

"What's *that* supposed to mean?"

"There aren't any TV cameras here, Andrea. Bill Hemmer isn't moderating. You can't debate me the way you debate Bob. I know you get paid to argue on TV, but I don't like you speaking to me like this. Millions of people aren't watching. You don't have to be right. In relationships, there doesn't have to be a winner and a loser. There are my feelings and your feelings; one isn't 'right' or 'wrong.' It's not always about *winning*."

Here is the most destructive casualty of misappropriated female power: it kills intimacy. The power that I was exerting was putting off any chance for a respectful reconciliation. After a humiliating, emasculating fight like that, Sam didn't want to be anywhere near me. No guy would. Intimacy? He was looking for a cotton bandage for his wounds, not silk sheets.

I had let my professional life bleed into my personal one and it was crushing someone I greatly cared for. Why was I fighting so hard? I wasn't winning *anything*. I was hurting someone's feelings. If anything, I was losing. My stomach sank.

I realized this wasn't some overnight process. I remembered my earlier boyfriend Weston. We had both been in our early twenties and worked for the same boss on Capitol Hill, which added a whole new layer of competition (another surefire intimacy killer). The more I thought about my fights with Weston, the more I remembered how hurtful I'd been to him during arguments. I wasn't respectful, nor was I considerate. I recalled the times when he would look at me, brokenhearted and in shock, and mutter, "I can't believe you just said that to me."

I felt horrible when I remembered it, and I still do. He loved me so much that I resorted to poorly thought-out, extreme measures when I wanted to end our relationship. I made a calculated decision to deliberately act like the biggest jerk on the planet one evening. I figured he'd be so appalled by me that he'd have no choice but to leave and fall out of love with me. After a few too many wines and a blowup that lasted hours, we found ourselves breaking up in a booth at Clyde's of Georgetown.

"I would have stayed forever," Weston told me, "but after last night I can't be with you."

I nodded, sick to my stomach and embarrassed. My plan had worked. I'd gotten exactly what I wanted: freedom. So why did I feel so terrible? In hindsight, it didn't have to be that way. A mature conversation would have been much better than having him hate me. I didn't need to disrespect him enough to drive him away. (Weston, if you're reading this, I'm very sorry.)

Even though the sexes are different, they both deserve respect.

I call it the Justice Scalia approach. You can engage in vigorous, heated debate as long as it doesn't get personal. If you assume good will, meaning that any disagreement is coming from a place where you aren't trying to deliberately hurt anyone, you can work through anything. Always, when possible, use humor. Though Sam and Weston were far from perfect (and I hardly was myself), they didn't deserve to be humiliated. What they taught me is that women who crush their guys with misapplied power find themselves alone. I took that lesson to heart. These days I haven't been alone for long and I'm much happier in my relationships—and so are the men I've dated.

Some guys *can* appreciate a strong woman, but they can't tolerate a disrespectful one. Nor should they. Strong women wouldn't tolerate it if their men acted the same way. This enormous loss of intimacy leads to things like infidelity, divorce, and men resorting to porn. Rather than fighting back, men choose to opt out of relationships. "The women in the pornos don't talk back to me," a male friend once told me. "I don't have to put up with their crap."

Another guy confessed to me that he cheated because his mistress didn't make him feel worthless like his wife constantly did. Does that justify cheating? Absolutely not. But restoring respect in relationships goes a long way toward keeping couples happy and happily committed. Intimacy isn't just about romance; it can also affect closeness between friends. If I had continued to beat up Bob Beckel in a way that wasn't civil, our friendship would have been over—and with good reason.

Sam's words showed me that I had to change. Just because you're being real doesn't mean you aren't being a real jerk. You can be authentically wrong. I realized that my potency is something I needed to be acutely aware of and something to apply *selectively*. If men shouldn't be brutes, how much worse is it when women are?

If we women want men to treat us well, then we must return

that respect. Our newfound female rights don't give us the right to trample all over them like doormats. Feminists tell women that we don't have to apologize for our power (or for anything else, for that matter). But that isn't the case. If one sex is always favored to win, then both sexes lose. It's the reason why some women will stay forever single. Life isn't Burger King. *You can't have it your way all the time.*

I cringe when I hear lines like "I knew I married Mrs. Right; I just didn't know she'd be right all the time!" It implies that the man has become neutered and the woman is infallible. Is that what any woman actually wants in her husband? A "yes man"? Have we replaced Stepford wives with Stepford husbands? Another one that makes my stomach turn is "Happy wife, happy life!" Shouldn't both partners' happiness be important? If you want someone to boss around and berate, get a dog. Most men won't hang around to be a punching bag, and those who do will surely be unhappy— and nothing ruins a relationship like an unhappy partner. By focusing so much on part of the partnership, feminists have gotten to the point where they've thrown the dynamic out of whack.

In 1970, women's lib pioneer Susan Brownmiller told *New York* magazine that "[w]omen as a class have never subjugated another group. We have never marched off to wars of conquest in the name of the fatherland. Those are the games men play. We see it differently. We want to be neither oppressor nor the oppressed."

What a crock.

Feminists like Brownmiller did march off to war: one against men. Their conquest was the patriarchy, and they won by overthrowing it and assuming it in the name of the motherland. They didn't want to merely tinker with the gender disparity; they wanted to make men pay for it. Today the scales are culturally tipped in the other direction. Women aren't rising up with their own female power, but are simply adopting the masculine version of it.

For decades women have tried to change the worst parts of men. The trope is that a husband bosses his "ball and chain" around: "Honey, where's my dinner?" "Iron my pants!" "Get me a sandwich!" The husband got the first, last, and every other word, while the dutiful wife was relegated to the kitchen, where she belonged. Today a man ordering his wife around would be viewed as a national scandal. But in this new era of female power, the rules have changed in favor of females, and sadly the roles have been swapped. Author and activist Warren Farrell points out, "If a man belittles a woman, it could become a lawsuit. If women belittle men, it's a Hallmark card."

We still talk all the time about how to address men overpowering women—and we should. Yes, there are instances of men being too dominant all over the place and acting like nitwits. But talk to most younger men and they'll tell you that they're acutely aware of how they speak to women. Instances of men being downright sexist are fewer and farther between than in the 1950s. I've noticed a significant drop in overt sexism, mainly because society largely doesn't tolerate it (except on Twitter and social media it seems). But our culture is okay with *men* getting mistreated. Men aren't wired to play the victim and to speak up. They won't really pen editorials about it or organize marches.

This sexism-in-a-skirt is the politically correct form of dominance these days, where women assert unchecked power over males both professionally and personally. Rather than seeking an even playing field of mutual respect, women have adopted the worst part of the guys. We boss them around and always have to win every argument. *Pursuing* happiness? No, we *demand* it.

Why have so many women taken on the same characteristic that we so hated about men? In my view, it's because the women's rights movement has increasingly become based in revenge and anger, alongside a belief that women are the superior sex. Any-

time you have one race, gender, or ethnicity believing that it's
better, you're going to have an oppressor and an oppressed. Culturally it's becoming more evident that women are the new men
and men are being billed as the weaker sex, instead of our equals.

This subordination of men by women is played out on television screens across America. As one *Men's Health* writer put it,
"The idiot dad has been a stereotype for as long as I can remember, despite research showing that fathers are more engaged with
kids, and better at raising them than ever before. So why are TV
dads such buffoons?"

Much of it has to do with the fact that television audiences are
mostly female. The content-producers are marketing to a movement. Millions of dollars are spent in market research to make
shows that people want to watch. But why would women want
to see men being belittled? I asked this very question of a marketing executive. He told me that in a way it's revenge for all the
frustration that females feel at work and at home. "Women are
stressed out and overwhelmed. It's their way of fighting back.
Plus it's better than having the woman looking stupid in their
eyes." But who are these women who want to be in relationships
with a buffoon? I suppose some women like to dominate a submissive, but that's typically in a dungeon in head-to-toe leather.
Most women claim to want mutual respect.

Culturally, I can point to many influences on my generation.
Look at icons like Madonna, simulating sex as if she were a man
and dominating dozens of submissive male dancers around her.
I recall watching Demi Moore in *G.I. Jane* infamously shout out
"Suck my dick!" Sure it was a movie, but I've heard many women
use the phrase over time. Why do women feel they need to have
a penis to exude power? An honest man once told me having a
penis is a constant disadvantage. Besides, women carry around
the most powerful weapon with us everywhere we go. Why are

we envying and emulating the guys? You'd never hear a man say "Suck my boob." It just wouldn't happen.

Like it or not, there are certain behaviors that are overwhelmingly male: Urinating outside. Burping. Manspreading. Even Benjamin Franklin wrote an essay urging men to "fart proudly." These are things that women absolutely are physically capable of doing, but that will never be acceptable female behavior in society. God help us if they ever are!

Let's take the case of Bethenny Frankel. Bethenny was a breakout star from *The Real Housewives of New York*, a reality series about a bunch of often-neurotic and usually obnoxious women. They played out the drama in their lives for our viewing pleasure while drinking chardonnay at fancy restaurants. Bethenny's macho mannerisms and tough talk made her famous. Just like Demi Moore, during one episode Bethenny chided her fellow housewife to "get off her jock" and later told another housewife to "blow me." Demi Moore's character was trying to fit into a male group, but Bethenny was surrounded by females. Even as successful a woman as her felt that she had to act like a man to win an argument and appear strong. That defeats the entire point of female empowerment.

Bethenny eventually found love during her TV tenure. The perpetual bachelorette met Jason, a seemingly kind man who could both challenge her intellectually and compete in the witty repartee department. They soon married and had a child. The series *Bethenny Getting Married* was followed by *Bethenny Ever After*. What people remember most about the wedding wasn't her dress or her veil or her vows. No, it was the fact that she couldn't make it to the bathroom before the service because then the guests would see her dress. Her solution? She peed in a bucket, on camera, for her friends, family, fiancé, and future children to see.

The etiquette books make clear that it's bad form to be seen in your wedding dress before the ceremony. But none of them address peeing in a bucket (on national television!), because the very idea would have been unthinkable not that long ago. It's typical of a guy to pee outside or in a random spot. Even in a bridal gown, Bethenny still acts like a man through and through. She's confrontational and foul-mouthed, needlessly so. She pushes people around in a bullying sort of way that is far more masculine than feminine. In fact, there are very few feminine aspects of Bethenny that I can cite. She's *macho*.

As Bethenny channeled more testosterone than most women and even some men, it wasn't until after the wedding and her new baby that the cameras uncovered a really ugly side of her marriage. Tantrums, tears, meltdowns, and fighting ensued almost daily. She belittled her husband in front of the cameras every chance she got. She was controlling, rude, and treated him like an employee instead of an equal. It's one thing to have more nerve than your husband; it's another to use it to publicly demean him on your own show. Sadly this marks a growing trend among women. Rather than having uncivilized, boorish behavior typically reserved for cads, it's *women* who have become the new Neanderthals. Just look at the movies being made that try to normalize and fuel this raunchy behavior: *Trainwreck*, with Amy Schumer, and *How to Be Single*, which features a promo of the main actress borderline blacked out. It's like we're deliberately trying not to be male and female.

But there's hope. There was hope for me and there was hope for Bethenny. Maybe it was watching the demise of her marriage play out on national television that softened her. After coming out of hiding to promote a new book, she told Bravo's Andy Cohen that she now writes about mutual respect. "I think that people should be in relationships with people that really accept and understand them."

She went on to reference the power struggle between men and women and "how hard it is when the woman is the breadwinner. Fame and attention and money doesn't bring out the best in everybody. Money is the root of all evil." Close but no cigar—not even a Virginia Slims. There is no better example of a woman who supports and elevates her husband than the traditional woman of means. It's not the money that's the problem; it's the *power*.

Bethenny and I each had our own "aha" moments. We learned that power can ruin relationships and destroy intimacy both on and off camera. It was refreshing to hear a softened Bethenny recognize that mutual respect is necessary. It reminded me of my exchange with Sam. As human beings we all have to learn that lesson or else we'll never be happy in our personal or professional relationships. But it's quite sad that this needed to be an epiphany, and at such a late age—and at the cost of a marriage.

I empathize with Bethenny. It *is* hard as a successful woman to find a man who is secure enough in his own skin to handle it. I've had past boyfriends struggle with being the secondary breadwinner when their careers weren't flourishing at the time that mine was. Yes, it was their issue and not mine. But it was still an issue in *our* relationship.

Steve Harvey makes the same point in this way: men can't be what women want them to be until they're where they need to be in their own professional lives. The women who have the strongest relationships are sensitive to the fact that we've made a trade. They realize Harvey's observation that men need to be in the right place before they get married. They need to feel like they have a career, that they can provide. If men don't have a job, Harvey points out, and they can't pay the bills and provide for the women in their family, then they're not getting married. Yet regardless of how comparatively well the woman might be doing, there's never any justification to beat the man down.

The feminist argument is that men have all the power. Every week it seems as if there are new surveys and studies competing to paint the most pathetic possible picture of modern masculinity. Today men are seen as skinny-jean-wearing, overly emotional man-children who are pushed to be in touch with their emotions—only to be ridiculed when they do so. Men are more metrosexual than ever before, increasingly becoming like women in their obsession with appearance. Plastic surgery rates among guys have seen an enormous uptick, as has greater male devotion to manscaping and hygiene. Men appear to be confused about what they are and un-sure about who they're meant to be. With more of them feeling disenfranchised, disillusioned, and disempowered, isn't it possible to think of men as the new marginalized minority? Might men, in fact, be the new women? And, if so, who's to blame for making them feel so mediocre? Time for our man-in-the-mirror moment, girls. We're a big part of the problem.

We want our guys to watch *The Notebook* with us but we get mad when they ignore us for the football game. We want men to be manly—as long as it doesn't require wearing that T-shirt we don't like or putting their feet up on our couch. We gripe about them leaving the seat up but leave bottles of hair products and makeup all over the sink, creating an even bigger mess. We tell men we like it when they take the lead, but when they pick the "wrong" restaurant we criticize their choice and make a new plan.

We took much of the power from men, many of their traits, and stopped acting like women. We instructed men that we could pay our bills, open our own doors, and carry our own bags. It's all about us, and we're the ones who need constant and total control. Of course women don't like to be treated like second-class citizens—*but neither do men.*

Smart, strong women have always been considered attractive. What has changed is how we use that strength. Rather than using it to build men up and to support them, we've used it to tear them down and push them around. Can it be considered a woman's world if we're acting like men? Have we really made inroads if we're constantly comparing ourselves to the opposite sex and regarding their role as the better one? We need to play *our* game, not *theirs*.

I'm proud to be a woman. I love all the things that come with it: hair, makeup, the fact that we overshare our emotions and obsess about first-date outfits for days. If women are as proud of their gender as we say we are, then why aren't more females embracing it? Nowadays the adjective "girly" is a kiss of death. It insinuates conforming to an outdated norm, from when women weren't equal. There's also an implicit directive that makes us women feel like we're being lectured and talked down to.

As someone who doesn't exactly like being told how to act, I can see why women shun the expression "act like a lady." Letting men be chivalrous isn't easy, especially if you're a strong woman who likes to be in control. It means sitting back and acting like a lady in the traditional sense while the man steps up, in that same traditional sense. As the *Atlantic* put it in their article about this "Lady-bro" phenomenon, these days "there is no pressure for a girl to be a girl." Men aren't being allowed to hunt, which is their natural urge. Women are acting even *worse* than men in their behavior. Movies like *Bridesmaids* and *How to Be Single* send the okay to women to act like completely belligerent, boorish, slovenly pigs—something that is attractive to no man. These movies should be titled *How to Stay Single*.

The phrase "playing like a girl" similarly has a negative connotation. A girl is weak. She doesn't play the game well and isn't as strong as the guys. "Girly girl" is another phrase that sounds condescending. But men have used it to describe me many times. A date once told me, "You are *such* a girly girl. I love it." All I had done was fix my makeup. Just the basic act of putting on lipstick has somehow become rare and exotic, something to apologize for.

Girls had and continue to have an enormously powerful hand—but we can play it wrong by playing like a guy. I've observed professional women feeling pressure to learn about sports so they can keep up with the guys, rather than admit to watching the season finale of *The Bachelor* for fear of appearing too "girly." I can remember all the women in Washington, D.C., I knew who felt that they had to hit the golf course or the cigar bar to not miss out on any potential political deals. It's one thing if a woman genuinely likes sports, but it's another if she feels like she has to artificially man up in order to succeed.

In relationships it's the woman who traditionally green-lights the first meeting. It's she who accepts the invite and who okays intimacy, she who controls when they have sex and its frequency. This is the epitome of female power applied correctly. Such power shouldn't be squandered in an effort to play like a guy. Guys have no filter, no red light. When it comes to sex their light is always bright green. *Women civilize men.*

Steve Harvey wrote a wildly popular book called *Act Like a Lady, Think Like a Man* (not *Act Like a Man, Think Like a Man*). Like me, Harvey is convinced that being a girl is a lost art form and something that females need lessons in. "Appreciating a man, not undermining his confidence, is the best way to get the best out of your guy," he argues. "And the best way to appreciate him is by being a girl, and especially letting him be a man." Don't tell him where you like to go. Let him figure out a place. Despite what feminism claims, it's hardly oppression if you're *choosing* to let him pick.

Men enjoy feeling like the hunter. It's in their DNA. There's nothing weak in letting a man call you first. There's also nothing wrong with inviting a shy guy to a party, which should be all the cue he needs to request that true first date. If you ask Patti Stanger, the Millionaire Matchmaker, the number one commandment in relationships is "Thou shalt act like a lady." This means being polite and saying things like "please," "thank you," and "excuse me." Men admire, trust, and respect women with class. This includes respecting his space and not calling or emailing him excessively, and it definitely includes not getting belligerently drunk.

Acting like a lady also includes not being the man in the relationship. By this I'm specifically referring to the trope where the woman takes the lead on the date: planning it, paying for it, and pursuing sex after it. Stanger warns it's a recipe for disaster. It's also a veiled attempt at total control, and control goes back to power. When one party holds all the power, the relationship has little hope for survival. *Misused power in any kind of relationship destroys intimacy.*

In society today, figures like Harvey and Stanger are hailed as geniuses. They aren't exactly breaking new ground or reinventing the wheel. In fact, they're just highly logical and in tune with the problems that are tying men and women in knots. They're nontraditional messengers, to be sure, but their messages are traditional ones. These are the lessons that so many prematurely discarded as "outdated," leading to a lack of guidance in return.

As a type-A woman with power, a good job, and a big bank account, I admittedly find it hard to always stay feminine amid so many traditionally masculine qualities. Women have certainly assumed a more aggressive tone when dealing with men. We've been told to go after them much like they do us. But each time I've experimented with sending a forward text, it didn't result in the outcome that I wanted. Instead, it was inevitably read as something sexual. As my big brother always says, "If a guy wants to spend time with you, he will make it happen." So true.

I'll gladly admit that I used to like to be chased by guys when I was single. I think most women do. I like when men court me, call me, pick the dinner spot, and pay the tab. I'm old-fashioned and unapologetic about it. And while this experiment backed up my hypothesis that traditional gender roles are best when you're dating, it made me wonder why so many women feel that they need to be the man. Does it go back to that inability to turn off the professional power switch? Besides being uncomfortable for me, I found it exhausting. As Caitlyn Jenner joked during her ESPYs speech, it's hard enough figuring out what to wear.

There's been many an instance where I've taken control in a playful way behind closed doors. This can be sexy and hot. But on a daily basis it can be wiener-shriveling. As Stanger puts it, women who are too take-charge and controlling do not "inspire boners." Stanger says that he who pays becomes "the man," and that by picking up the bill the woman takes the guy's job away. For years we were told to split checks and that it was okay to pay. Yes, down the road if you're in a serious relationship it's fine now and then, but at the very beginning it's the man who should pay. For many men, splitting a first date check is a clear signal from the woman that she isn't interested in him. She's implying that she doesn't want to accept that meal lest he "get ideas."

During the push for feminism we shirked our "lady duties" in favor of proving a point: that we could do what the men could. But why, and to what end? Harvey says we shouldn't do any heavy lifting, or fix anything like the toilet or a car. Those are the guy's jobs. Frankly, what woman would want to do that anyway? I had a boyfriend who never let me touch the trash. He didn't love garbage; he liked to feel like the man. Watching me do it, he said, made him feel like less of one. It made him feel good to do manly things. I wasn't gonna argue—especially with my new manicure. That's one very easy way for powerful women to let regular guys feel like equals. Men need to feel like they're bringing something to the table.

Rather than keep some of the timeless traditions of the past, we've gutted them altogether and watched the pendulum swing the other way. Women used to be the ones who did the grocery shopping, made the meals for the family, balanced the checkbook, and did the laundry. But many of the problems that women face in society today exist because feminists denounced and devalued the important roles of homemakers and mothers. By throwing away these roles, today's women often have no idea how to manage finances, cook, clean, and do laundry. I have a friend who is a professional organizer, who argues that those decisions were the very reason why we have such high childhood obesity rates and credit card debt nowadays. It's why "professional organizer" has become a profession, something that would have been laughable in earlier times.

While women wrestle with whether or not they should act like ladies in their private lives, we're equally tied up in knots about how to maintain our femininity and be taken seriously at work. Women who have gone before me will tell you that they had to act and dress like men to get ahead. Study after study sent women mixed messages on how to act in a professional setting: "Be nice but not too nice." "Make suggestions but don't talk too much." "Don't get angry, get focused." "Whatever you do, don't cry!"

While men don't have these issues, women seemingly can't win. A report titled "Damned if You Do, Doomed if You Don't" surveyed 1,231 senior executives from the United States and Europe. It found that women who act in ways that are consistent with gender stereotypes—defined as focusing "on work relation-

ships" and expressing "concern for other people's perspectives"—
are considered less competent. But if they act in ways that are
seen as more "male"—like "act assertively, focus on work tasks,
display ambition"—they are seen as "too tough" and "unfemi-
nine." *The Feminine Mystique* has now become quite the feminine
critique, with women under the gun in ways that men simply
aren't. Rather than ushering in equality, a double standard has
come into existence—and it's not going away anytime soon.

A 2015 Arizona State University study said pretty much the
same thing. Men and women, whether at work or on a jury, are
not equally in a position to express anger. Men can pound the
table and seem fired up. If I pounded the table people would say
that I have anger issues. Men can ask for more money with ease,
while women are often intimidated to do the same—and called
greedy if we do. Men are constantly competing with other men.
If I try to get promoted I'm a throat-slitter. Men can relay info
and trade porn passwords at a business lunch, but when women
chat it's gossip or "typical girl stuff." Men can railroad other men
or not get along with other guys in the office. If a female doesn't
love everyone then she's mean. Utterly effective at your job? Well,
then you must be bossy.

In professional settings women tend to have less ego and are
able to build consensus much faster. Though we can be more
emotional, we are also more compassionate and caring—valuable
traits when it comes to building a team. When I worked on Capitol Hill for House GOP conference chairman Deborah Pryce, I
observed how fast the female lawmakers on both sides of the aisle
could come together to turn an idea into legislation.

Getting a bill through Congress is a very long process. First,
the rep gets the idea that there's a problem and decides that
they're the one who can fix it. They draft the legislation, working

with all these different groups. They work on language, and they work on policy. Then the legislation actually gets crafted. The congressperson starts to get support in the media, and then gets support on Capitol Hill. It's fascinating to observe.

Whenever there's a women's issue, the (bipartisan) Congressional Caucus for Women's Issues immediately rallies the female members of the House and the Senate. It's not a pissing contest with the women; women aren't biologically equipped for that. Most of the time, these congresswomen just want solutions. When one member has a domestic violence bill or similar type of legislation, the others generally rally around to help her. Yes, they can be huge monsters, but they still generally support each other.

Congresswoman Pryce always told the story of how they put all the female politicians in a room and figured out the problem behind violence-against-women legislation literally within an hour—unheard-of by Washington standards. That's how she got a number of women to support us on the End Demand for Sex Trafficking Act of 2005. The congresswomen were efficient and outcome based, shelving their egos. The male members, on the other hand, would hoot and holler and pound their chests. This extended outside Congress, too.

So why are women trying to be in the boys' club? Obviously the women who've gone before us had to play in a guy's world to succeed. Today there should be more focus on going back to what we know best and *do* best, even if it's neither easy nor easily accepted. Women have skills men don't, and it's delusional to pretend that those skills don't exist or are somehow inherently inferior.

The majority of women I know like when men act like men, and men like when women act like women—and look like them, too. Call it sexist, call it misogynistic. Call it whatever the hell you want. I call it *reality*. Put a woman in high heels and a soft, flirty dress next to a woman in a manly pantsuit with flats, and the man is naturally drawn to the softer-looking gal. We're detached from reality if we're somehow pretending that men aren't visual creatures who like to look at women a certain way.

I tend to dress in a way that my man likes. If he prefers heels, I'll wear heels. If he prefers boots, I'll wear boots. If he hates the color orange, I likely won't be wearing an orange dress on our date. This doesn't make me a weak woman; it makes me a smart one. Don't we all ask our girlfriends for fashion advice? Why is it bonding to take their views into consideration, but subordination to go along with your partner? If I'm wearing his favorite dress then he is excited all evening. Doesn't this benefit me in the end and make us both happy?

Look at *Modern Family* star Sofia Vergara. It's no coincidence that the highest-paid actress in television *embraces* her feminine side. She dresses for men and plays up her female assets, though not in a slutty, pornographic way. She's so family-friendly she has a line of clothes in Kmart. Vergara doesn't get into sharing nude photos on Instagram or overshare about her sex life. She keeps the mystery by conserving the intimacy, which makes her even sexier. She took off from work to take care of her then boyfriend, hunky Joe Mangianello. This is something that women would be impugned for in most major magazines.

You're supposedly not a strong woman unless you're walking all over your man. But when you're paid the most in your industry, you're the alpha female by definition. It takes more courage for Vergara and others to fight the cultural trend against femininity than it does to conform to a more masculine version of how women are told to act. Staying true to feminine urges isn't always easy, but it certainly fits the description of feminism better than trying to play in a man's world.

Writer Heidi Basarab confessed in the *New York Times* that her mother wanted more for her than "just" being a housewife. These types of mothers care for their daughters just as much as mine did, but the women's movement made it seem that we had to make a choice. When Basarab decided that she wanted to marry her boyfriend after ten years, she had to break the news to her mom. From the way she writes, it literally would have been easier for her to come out as a lesbian than to admit that she wanted to be married.

"Telling her felt like a betrayal," she wrote. "When I was growing up, she repeatedly and vehemently said I didn't need to get married, didn't need a man, didn't need anybody to take care of me. This mantra carried so much weight in my childhood it was almost physical, as if she had braided it into my pigtails, sprinkled it across the buttered layers of potato strudels she baked, and knotted it into the smocked pinafores she sewed. But it turns out, I didn't need a man. Instead, it turned out I needed one particular man. It took me a ridiculously long time to recognize the difference."

We all *want* a good man, whether we *need* them or not. There's no shame in admitting that you want to be in a loving relationship. Yet for many feminists that sounds flawed, like the woman is saying her existence is incomplete. But if no man is an island, surely no woman is, either.

While we are wired one way, men are, too, in their own way. They need to feel like providers, as Harvey says. They need to demonstrate their chivalrous side so that they feel needed. Feminists collectively moan when they hear this. They often jump to the conclusion that this means we women should change how we want to act or dumb ourselves down so that men can feel big and

strong. But that's not what Stanger or Steve Harvey is saying—
and neither am I. It's okay to want to care for a man and be cared
for, even though so many daughters have been discouraged from
choosing that path.

My mom encouraged me to be strong yet feminine. She
knew that the two characteristics can absolutely coexist without
a woman having to compromise anything. Being true to your
natural female urges, being authentic, is truly powerful—and a
pathway to peace of mind.

Alternative music was really big when I was in tenth grade,
and all the girls were wearing baggy jeans and T-shirts to school.
I didn't even bother trying to pull off that sort of look, but my
mom said, "How you dress affects how you behave. You have all
these cute sundresses. Wear them with some sandals and just see
what happens. Why don't you experiment and try dressing more
feminine?" How sad it is that encouraging someone to be "feminine" is frequently taken as an offense nowadays. That doesn't
sound like the love of female power to me.

So I wore my sundress with some light makeup and my hair
down, and Mom was right. I walked into Mrs. Herbert's Spanish
class and caught the eye of a group of senior football players. I got
so much attention that day that I wore sundresses for the rest of
high school. I wasn't dressed provocatively. I wasn't even in heels.
The sundress came to my knee. It was flowy without showing
cleavage. It wasn't that I was showing skin. It was that I was
displaying *femininity*. The power was still mine, not theirs. I wish
all women had the helpful guidance that I did.

Female power is amazing. Why did we trade so many aspects of
it to be like the guys? The goal should be fairness, preserving the
strengths of our dissimilarities, cherishing the power that comes
through being a woman and not in spite of being one. A first-
rate woman can only ever be a second-rate man. We can reach

our career and family goals by staying true to our natural needs and desires—without trying to keep up with, emulate, or imitate men. But that can only be achieved through authenticity, not ideology. Rather than manning up, it's time we got comfortable playing like a girl.

Chapter 4

On Tying the Knot

I NICKNAMED HIM Uncle Rico, and I thought we were going to be married. After all, that's what he had promised me time and again.

For almost three years I did nothing but be a great girlfriend to him. I cooked for him and supported him—and he did the same for me. We made a good couple. And a couple we stayed, month after month after month. After a while I began to wonder if he actually had any interest in marrying me at all. Rather than listen to what people say, it's critical to watch what they *do*. I became convinced that he didn't want to get hitched. Finally I reached my breaking point. After hearing from the neighbor, the cleaning lady, and the rumor mill that he had decided he never wanted to get married but just hadn't shared the news with me, I decided to ask him point-blank one weekend on vacation. For some reason he wasn't acting like himself. As we sat at a wine bar shortly after brunch it just hit me: ask him. Ask him the question you have asked him before. Ask him again. Now.

I looked right into his eyes, tilted my head and gently said, "Do you want to get married? Please. I'm begging you, please don't lie to me."

He paused for a while. He made a face I had never seen before, like he knew he couldn't lie anymore. And for some reason, I knew that this time, his answer would finally be honest. "I don't." The words cut me to my core. And I should have known better.

I'm not going to be with someone who doesn't want to be with me, or who doesn't have the same goals as I do. That's a waste of time. Despite his pleas to stay and give him more time, I wasn't prepared to lose myself for one more day.

In the months that followed, as I grieved our uncoupling, I found that I hadn't just moved on from the life I had with Uncle Rico. Part of me had also moved on from the idea of marriage as a life goal. The more I thought about it, the more I thought that maybe marriage wasn't for me, either.

I admit it: I had a love/hate relationship with marriage. There was a time in my teens when I fantasized about my wedding, like every little girl does. But as I got older, my career fantasies eclipsed my personal ones. I delighted in the thought of saying "I do" . . . to my dream job. By the time my father passed away in 2009, any rare daydream I had about walking down the aisle just vanished. I loved the idea of my dad giving me away, and dancing with him at the reception. I hated the reality that it would never happen with him gone. Somehow when he died my desire for a wedding did, too. Uncle Rico had given me a spark of hope, but never the big wedding itself. (I had even considered eloping.) When we parted ways, I took marriage and put it at the end of my list of priorities. I finally realized that the love knot should be strong enough to hold two people together, not confine or hold one of them back. When you tie the knot, it has to be perfect, or it will hurt you. The friction will burn you, or it will fall apart. But when it's right, it can bind and secure you in a way you never thought possible. And like any knot, you'll know when it's tied right.

I love the idea of having that one person who can be your best friend, whom you share your hopes and dreams with, whom you grow old with. I do want that one person who always has my back and loves me unconditionally, in sickness and in health, for richer or poorer, till the day I die.

I take commitment seriously. If I say that I'm going to do something, I do it. I was raised to be a woman of her word, a woman who keeps her promises and doesn't make ones she can't fulfill. This is but one of several reasons why I was hesitant to jump into holy matrimony. For me, a divorce would feel like a failure—and in my worldview failure is not an option. I've seen the pain it can cause. The Bible compares it, and for good reason, to a tearing of the flesh after two people are joined together and then separated. That is, effectively, how much it hurts. I've been divorce adjacent, when my sister was going through hers. It's brutal.

As someone whose feet are firmly placed in reality, I also know the statistics are against me. The broad statistical consensus was that the likelihood of me being in a healthy, working marriage was slim to none—and slim had just left town. Divorce is everywhere. Everywhere you look, people are splitting up. I don't kid myself for a second when it comes to monogamy. I think it can be very challenging for some women, and especially for men. Comedian Eric Loco once tweeted, "My son asked me what marriage is like. I told him to delete every song on his iPod except one." The takeaway: Pick a really good song that you really like. You may get sick of it sometimes, but you will always love it.

Even though people can choose a song, they end up sneaking off to listen to other artists. When news broke that Ashley Madison—a website established to enable adultery—was hacked, I just felt sad. Deception is running rampant and so is adultery. Doesn't anyone keep their promises anymore? Why get married if you don't want to be committed?

For the previous fifteen years I knew that I wanted to make my career a priority. I fully understood at various points in the past that I couldn't say the vows to my boyfriend, simply because I wouldn't be able to uphold them. It's too bad that more people don't think this way. Again, as a society, we don't seem to want to honor our agreements—which leads to the question of why so many people pretend to commit in the first place.

Picking a partner is the most important decision a woman makes in her life. The wrong choice will alter a lifetime personally and professionally—and profoundly. Sheryl Sandberg stressed a similar point in *Lean In*: "I truly believe that the single most important career decision that a woman makes is whether she will have a life partner and who that partner is." Because it's a conservative message, the mainstream media conveniently missed that paragraph from her book.

Partnership is like a soufflé: when you get it right it's amazing, but if you screw it up it can be awful. I think a lot of people get married for the wrong reasons. It can be family pressure, or because their friends are doing it, so like sheep they follow. Others simply want to check a box to silence the ticking clock. I've been to my share of weddings and heard the bride admit things like, "Am I in love with him? No, but he'll make a good father." Or, "Everyone else was getting married. I just couldn't be the last one." One bride even admitted to me on her wedding day that her groom wasn't the love of her life but that he had "good sperm" for mating. Ah, romance.

The more weddings I attended, the more petrified of marriage I became. The more married couples I talked to, the more I questioned if marriage was something I wanted. I don't want to control a man, or be controlled. I don't want to have to marry a man because I need him; I want to marry him because I want *him*. I need to be in a situation where, as my good friend Victoria once said, "you simply cannot imagine your life without that one person, or missing one moment of your future with him." That's the kind of love I want. It's the kind we should all want and hold out for. And I'm glad I did, because it finally paid off.

A friend once told me that marriage should be the easiest decision you ever make, if you find the right one. She was right. Of course people should be able to chart their own course. But as a professional observer of culture, I can't help but notice an iceberg of social misery straight ahead—and we as a country are traveling full speed ahead into it. I understand the weight of expectations and the disappointment felt by both girls and guys. I've heard the stories of horror and I've watched our relationships regress instead of progress.

For most of my life, I believed that marriage was a wonderful goal. It was something that I grew up wanting to have. But many things along the way have slowly caused me to doubt the institution itself. Like many of my contemporaries, my certainty has been diluted by skepticism. The first bit of doubt came when I dated a divorcé. Listening to his stories of horror, hearing how he had been cheated on after a decade of supposed marital bliss, left me slightly jaded. But still I was largely optimistic.

Then came Uncle Rico and being led on for years, as he held out the promise of marriage and children despite having no interest in either. He constantly made digs at the institution. "Marriage is just a license to live a woman's life," he once said.

"But our relationship isn't like that," I replied.

"Yeah, but you women change."

"If I haven't changed after three years I won't change after we get married." I argue for a living. I thought I could change his mind, since I was convinced that I was speaking the truth. Uncle Rico knew I was right; he wasn't giving me reasons to avoid marriage in general so much as making excuses to buy time for himself. Now I believe that if a man hasn't proposed after two years, it's almost certainly time for the woman to write him off and look for someone who shares her goals. As my brother Dean would say, "No man wins the lottery and waits two years to cash in the ticket."

Sadly, Uncle Rico's depredation wasn't unique. Once I picked up on what he was doing, I noticed this pattern appearing more and more often in my friends' relationships. When I was dating heavily on my Freedom Tour, at least half a dozen men confessed that they were petrified of getting married. They feared it was some sort of prison.

They weren't just immature and looking to sow their oats until the day they died. To my surprise, their concerns were often quite reasonable. The biggest one? "Nobody is faithful." Another told me that he felt that wives want to control everything that their husbands do—and then "melt their brains." That . . . doesn't sound very fun.

The most honest one simply had a blunt question: "How many married couples do you know who are truly happy?" When I was faced with doing the actual math, I came up short. As much as I wanted to inflate the number so that he would feel more reassured that it was a worthwhile endeavor, I struggled to come up with some names. To me, being truly happy means being in a state of more or less constant bliss. That doesn't sound like many marriages I know. Every single marriage that I was familiar with had tremendous challenges—and not just the challenges that come with marriage itself. I racked my brain and was able to come up with only three examples. That's not a huge proportion.

Would I trade places with the rest of the couples I knew? I asked myself. The more I thought about the question, the more I realized that none of these marriages was *clearly* preferable to my single-but-never-alone lifestyle.

I agree with the conservative view that a married family is the best option for raising kids. There's absolutely no question of that in my mind. I agree that falling marriage rates correlate with broader societal disintegration and dysfunction. I agree that more stable, married households will have enormous positive social and personal consequences for many Americans. I just don't think that making marriages work is as simple as, say, slashing the income tax. There's more to it than the stroke of a pen.

What many conservatives don't get is that a lot of people get married for the wrong reasons. If conservatives push marriage as the solution to all social problems, that's only going to be exacerbated. Despite temporary doubts, I'm a huge proponent of the institution of marriage in general. I also think it benefits men: they live longer, they are healthier, and their quality of life is better. (That is, depending on who they are married to.) I think it would be great if people could stay together forever like they used to in the old days. But I don't think that's realistic, and I think there needs to be a little bit more forgiveness for people who make bad decisions. *Everyone's a sinner, and everyone makes mistakes.*

Marriage is the quickest way to lift someone out of an economic sort of depression. But do I think that it's the end-all, be-all, that it should be the ultimate goal of everybody? Can I honestly say that if someone doesn't get married, then they're a bad person and a failure? Absolutely not—and it does a real disservice to assume that it's some sort of universal truth. Family pressures and getting older are both very bad reasons to lock into a lifelong partnership. Fear—of being alone, for example—is also a terrible but very common reason to get married. In fact it's a bad reason to make *any* decision.

It's odd that even though it's conservatives who are the ones pushing for marriage as social policy, there seems to be a universal consensus that all women want to be married and have kids. Society—which includes total strangers—gets to judge them on how, when, and if they achieve it. At a certain point in a woman's life something starts to happen that's almost like watching a movie play out. First, people silently wonder when she's getting married. Then they get worried—is it too late for our heroine? Does she not realize the danger she's in, a danger we in the audience are painfully aware of? Well, we'd better warn her!

That's when people start to incessantly ask her when she'll get married. No matter how successful she is professionally, no matter if she's already in a relationship, the question starts to get woven into conversations with all the smoothness and subtlety of sandpaper. I used to get asked all the time: "What about you? Do you think you'll ever get married?" Sometimes the questioner's face reflected general curiosity. Other times it displayed outright concern, as if I were dying.

As far as I can tell, there are a few different reasons why people ask these types of questions. First, it helps them categorize you and figure you out. Married people especially can't seem to understand being in your thirties and unmarried—and some are envious of those who appear happy with their extended single lives. My sister, Thea, pointed out another major reason: "People don't know what else to talk about." They can only think to ask the lowest common denominator of questions. Yes, it's a lazy way to shoot the bull—but most people are lazy when it comes to small talk. In essence, that's the difference between small talk and real in-depth conversation. Are you making sounds, or are you engaging in ideas? Finally, I suspect that many people pry because of sheer, uncontrollable nosiness. It's as if they can't help themselves.

None of those possibilities might be all that palatable, but they're hardly outrageous. What is outrageous is when people ask such questions in order to make women feel bad about themselves. One of my Fox hairdressers is in the enviable position of having been married to her high school sweetheart for almost twenty years. Sadly, it seems like many women do envy her, and since women can be very bitchy, she gets "Don't you ever get bored? Gosh, it must be so boring to be with the same guy!" So much for building each other up.

Occasionally this approach seeps into the media, and we see some cultural "wake-up call" for single women. The subsequent advice is allegedly designed to help us chart a course to marital bliss. In actuality it ends up having the opposite effect, striking panic and fear in the hearts of unmarried women everywhere.

Susan Patton, "the Princeton mom," became famous for writing a letter in the *Daily Princetonian* titled, "Advice for the Young Women of Princeton: The Daughters I Never Had." "You will never again be surrounded by this concentration of men who are worthy of you," she wrote. She therefore urged them to grab a husband along with a degree. Patton struck a cultural nerve. The letter went viral, becoming fodder on editorial pages and on television shows for days.

As a traditional-minded woman, I can't completely discount what Patton says. Statistically, she was speaking truth. But here's my issue with Patton: besides the obvious fact that most men aren't emotionally developed enough or ready to settle down at twenty-two or twenty-three, she assumes that women want to be married right out of college. Frankly, I don't know many who do—especially nowadays.

Patton's charge was that if women aren't married, we need to be (stat!) or else we're doomed. Personally I don't think Patton wanted to make women feel judged or crazy, but she did so nevertheless. While her advice was meant to help, it also whipped up guilt and horror in the minds of many young women . . . including me. As one professional colleague put it, "She had us all so spun out."

All the same old questions came back at me when I heard about her letter: Should I have spent more time trying to tie down my college boyfriend, rather than tying one on at the local tavern? More time trying to get to walking down the aisle instead of listening to Wu-Tang? I thought about it long and hard. Very quickly I realized the answer to the marriage question was no, I shouldn't have. I had zero regrets about my college years. I may have graduated without a husband, but I'd earned two degrees—and they served as very reliable breadwinners.

Naturally Patton got a book deal after all the commotion, and I eagerly read *Marry by Choice, Not by Chance* to see what else she had to say. Some of her thoughts were spot-on: Women should find men who aren't threatened by their capacity for greatness, and smart women need equally smart men. Avoid bad boys. Don't date married men. Others I questioned: Find someone your own age. Use your early twenties when you are most desirable to your best advantage. (Who's getting married at twenty-three?) In the absence of Mr. Right, she claims, settling for Mr. Good Enough is "settling smart." But who wants to settle? "Look for men in settings that are more organic than online or in singles bars." Great advice, if it were 1997. My personal favorite: "If you are a woman in her thirties redouble your efforts to find The One before it's too late!" Exclamation point! This is a *shemergency*!

Women put enough stress on themselves to get married. It's hard enough trying to find a quality man to date, let alone one to form a union with. *Who was this woman doling out this nerve-racking advice and generating such hysteria and fear?* I wondered. Hearing of my interest in what she was discussing, I soon received an email from Patton inviting me to grab drinks or dinner with her . . . and her divorced friend who had a complicated backstory. Clearly, this was meant to be a setup. While I passed on the matchmaking, I took her up on having a meal.

I wasn't thinking a sit-down would be a big deal one way or another. I meet all sorts of characters all the time on *Outnumbered*. But when I told one of my best friends about my plans, he was actually a bit worried for me. "She's going to try and make you feel bad about yourself," he insisted. "Be ready."

"You think?"

"Yes. You're thirty-five and not married. You put work first for the last decade, not men or marriage. Therefore, in her view, you messed up and you messed up big. She's going to try and scare you. Just be prepared."

He was right. It took only about five minutes into lunch for her to begin to interrogate me about my personal life: "I have to say, you are wildly successful, have this fabulous career . . . but you're not married. Do you want to get married someday?"

"Actually I'm single and I'm happy," I told her.

Patton looked confused . . . and then concerned. "Aren't you *worried?*"

I bit my tongue, even though I knew exactly what she'd meant. "About what?"

She tried to dance around the issue, as these types often do. "About . . . well . . . finding someone. You're thirty-five and, uh, very successful professionally but *personally . . .*" She didn't finish her thought. Instead she just made a face, and looked at me like I was in trouble.

Patton didn't realize that I was deliberately staying single and dating for the purpose of researching this book. I had just come out of two consecutive long-term relationships and needed some "me time." I also wanted to test my own convictions. If I'm going to be pro-marriage, surely it would make sense for me to check out the alternatives. What I learned almost immediately is that just because a woman isn't married doesn't mean that she's *alone*. Supposedly if there's no diamond on our ring finger, that means we're incomplete. In fact it's just the opposite.

I wasn't going to let Patton Princeton-mommy me, when my own mother doesn't mommy me. "No," I told her. "Being alone isn't something I fear. I'm cute, I'm fun, and I'm funny. I'll never be alone." (But not original—I stole that line from my sister.) It is sad that such female bravado usually only comes out when women are put on the spot, but it is also true. Desperation is the worst perfume and men can smell it a mile away. My confidence was what was attracting men to me, as it always had.

Patton wasn't buying it, and we discussed my relationship history for a bit. I even showed her a photo of an ex. He was very good-looking—but then, most vampires are. "Why on earth did you let *him* go?"

"It wasn't the right fit, for a lot of reasons. Look, I could have been married by now, and I could get married tomorrow. Getting married is easy. Marrying the right person is hard. Staying married is even harder."

Why did I feel the need to have to defend my decision to break up? Did I really owe it to a complete stranger who was making me so uncomfortable that I could barely enjoy chewing my Cobb salad? Why was I so busy trying to hint that he had been a liar, a fraud, and a phony who had intimacy issues? Why are we as women always explaining our choices? I didn't need to justify my choices to her or anybody else—and honestly, no woman does. Men never push and prod other men about their personal lives the way that women do when it comes to marriage and children.

As Patton sat there befuddled, shaking her head about why I would break up with someone who seemed fine, the interviewer in me wanted to turn the tables a bit. Who was this woman who was guilting me? And not just me, but the thousands of unmarried women who had read her book and ended up feeling judged? So turn the tables I did.

"What about you?" I asked. "What about your marriage?"

"I'm divorced."

Patton went on to tell me she married a man because she wanted to have kids, not because she was really in love with him. One day he left her and their boys and never came back. It was very sad to hear, and I felt bad for her. While she doled out advice to women on marrying smart, she was living proof of the ending that can take place when certain priorities are put above others. This is what commonly happens when you prefer checking the marriage box to getting it right (something she admits in her book).

Patton had made marriage a priority; I had not. We were both being true to ourselves. So why was only one of us in the hot seat? Shouldn't the real message be that, when it comes to marriage, women should follow their hearts regardless of age? Shouldn't putting other women on the spot about their decisions, pressuring them to make decisions based on *your* preferences, be outlawed? Patton presented a rosy picture of young love in her book that wasn't her actual reality. Didn't the author owe single women an authentic ending to her own advice?

It's true that college might be the most target-rich environment for a young educated woman. But that doesn't mean that getting married straight out of school is a must. You marry one person, not a statistical sample. Of course a woman should be aware of the doors that she is closing as she goes through life. But this applies to relationships as well as career and everything else.

"So are *you* seeing anyone?" I said.

"It's hard," she admitted. I knew where she was coming from.

If dating was hard for recent grads in their twenties, it must be hell for divorcées in their fifties. "I did just get asked out by Ben. He said you know him, actually."

"I do!" I told her. Ben was a famous author. "He's very, very smart. You should go."

She looked at me, repulsed. "He's so . . . *old.*"

"But he doesn't look it. And he's so accomplished!" I tried to mimic her advice that smart women need smart men, but deep down I wanted to ask the same questions that she had asked me: *Aren't you . . . scared? You know, to be alone?* Patton looked back at me but stayed silent. We both knew that what I said was true. For a moment I self-loathed for taking part in what I hated— namely, women putting other women on the spot.

It was then that I realized that Patton had been projecting from the very beginning. She wasn't afraid that I wouldn't be able to find a partner; she was afraid for herself. *She* was the one who was scared of being alone. There's a great deal of emphasis in our culture on being part of a duo. In my view, however, the real way to be part of a kick-ass team is to be two authentically comfortable parties of one.

The message that Patton should have given is: Choose the life that you want for yourself, regardless of what other women are doing—let alone telling you or scaring you to do. Satisfy your own expectations, not those of others. The minute we stop comparing ourselves to the woman next to us is the minute when we start to untie the knots.

"Love your solitude," Austrian poet Rainer Maria Rilke writes. Women need to be okay being alone. Of course that means loving yourself in the abstract, but it means it in practice as well. It means going to a wedding or a party by yourself, or taking a vacation by yourself. Some friends of mine are terrified to eat by themselves at a restaurant. Yet every single time I've been out, there has always been at least one person eating alone. Once you look for it, you see that it happens at literally every establishment. We don't even notice it because it's not a big deal—and there's no need to make it into one.

I understand that finding and maintaining a lasting relationship—especially the marital kind—seems like a harder endeavor now than at any point in the past. Talk to any young single woman and her fear and despondency come spilling out like rain on your wedding day: "I'm never getting married! Why is it taking me so long to find The One? Why can't guys just man up? I can't even get him to call me or take me on a real date, let alone get into a relationship. How will I ever find a man to marry? My mom was married with three kids by now! *What is wrong with me?*"

They're not being silly girls. There is somewhat of a marriage crisis right now—and it's women who are paying the price. Both men and women are waiting longer to marry or are not marrying at all. For girls in their thirties, finding a suitable partner who wants to settle down and have children can feel like *Mission: Impossible.* Many guys in their thirties want to date women in their twenties, making it slim pickings for the thirty-plus crowd.

What we want from our unions, why we want it, and how we go about getting it has never been more in flux than in recent years. According to bestselling author and marriage expert Stephanie Coontz, relationships have changed more in the past thirty years than in the previous three thousand. At the heart of these changes? Rising expectations. We've never expected more from our partners than we do right now.

Simply put, we as Americans want a lot—certainly more than our mothers or grandmothers ever thought possible. Many of us look at our parents' marriages with a kind of covert superiority, recognizing that what may have been good enough for mom isn't at all good enough for us. Things marriage was originally intended to provide, like social status and financial security, aren't the goal anymore—those are things we provide for ourselves beforehand.

When it comes to marriage, this generation of women is seeking nothing short of a superrelationship. We want a soulful, sexy, and inspired union that can help us realize our full potential in life. We want a deep connection with a best friend, an emotional and spiritual confidant, an intellectual counterpart who gets our inside jokes, matches us financially, and who loves us with a passion that rivals Romeo's. Women have gained power and are refusing to settle—and that is a good thing. Women can find that kind of love, but we just have to be patient enough to wait for it and refuse to settle for anything less than what we want: love, fidelity, kindness, respect. "You gotta give men something to come back for," my brother Dean always says. Women used to be the keeper of values. We can reclaim that role whenever we want. It is—and always has been—ours for the taking. Now *that* is feminine power.

Chapter 5

The Kindest Cut

WHO WOULD HAVE thought that sandwiches could be so controversial?

In the summer of 2015 *Glamour* published a column titled "13 Little Things That Can Make a Man Fall Hard for You." This one was different from other columns with similar headlines. We were used to being advised to be more confident or to receiving pointers on "sex to make his toes curl." *Glamour*'s article was filled with traditional advice, the sort of old-school wisdom I got from my mom.

Here's the list:

1. Stocking the fridge with his favorite drinks. Bonus points: Bring him back to his fraternity days by handing him a cold one as he steps out of the shower.

2. Making him a snack after sex. It doesn't have to be a gourmet meal—a simple grilled cheese or milk and cookies will do.

3. Emailing him the latest online gossip about his favorite TV show. You don't have to have a BFF at HBO. Just share applicable links from your Twitter feed and pat yourself on the back.

4. Bragging about him to your friends, family, the stranger on the street corner—whomever. Proclamations of pride will make his chest puff out and his heart swell.

5. Answering the door in a negligee—or, better yet, naked.

6. Being open to what he wants to try in the bedroom and out. An open mind is attractive no matter your playground.

7. Letting him solve your petty work problem. Many men don't gossip, but they do like to fix things.

8. Spitting out sports stats for his favorite team. Showing an interest in his favorite players will earn you points on and off the field.

9. Making a big deal out of his favorite meal. Does he like hot dogs cut up into his boxed mac and cheese? Serve it on a silver platter to really make him smile.

10. Treating his friends as well as you treat your own.

11. Sitting side by side while he vegs out to the TV. It may not feel like quality time to you, but it's the best time to him.

12. Giving him a massage—happy ending completely optional. In fact, a foot rub works just fine.

13. Taking him back to third grade with a gentle tease over anything from how you'll dominate him on the basketball court to the weird way he just styled his hair.

The feminist crowd was absolutely horrified. The magazine was impugned for publishing a "cringe-worthy," "antifeminist," "misogynistic" list. "*Glamour* thinks you should become a quasi-nonverbal sex robot in negligee," one feminist tweeted. "Fear not," wrote one female *Washington Post* columnist. "Since Eve, woman has been responsible for the fall of man, and again, we shall prevail." Women are always get dinged for overreacting. Now I see why. The response ranged from hyperbolic rants to hysteria at the idea that doing nice things could trigger . . . *the fall of man*? Good grief. Talk about missing the point.

Discussing the national outrage on *Outnumbered* only made it worse. God forbid we not join the chorus of feminists everywhere in ripping the column apart. Always opinionated on the couch, I was the only one who offered a fervent defense of the column as well intentioned. While I didn't love every idea, I did think some were worthwhile. "If your man is hungry after doing the 'horizontal hula,' make him a sandwich," I quipped. "What's so bad about that? That's not called the 1950s, that's called *kindness*."

Enter: Sandwichgate.

The blogs wasted no time putting me squarely in their crosshairs, giving *Glamour* a break as I acted as their flak jacket: "Fox News host to women: Let your man bang you, then feed him beer and food to thank him." The commenters only had more hyperbole, more word twisting—and more point missing: "You poor poor woman, I feel so sorry for your lack of self-esteem and self-worth!" "Is there anyone who believes Tantaros is that type of subservient woman? On appearances alone [!], I've always had her pegged as a high maintenance 'princess' sort, not the giving kind." No wonder we haven't been able to have an honest discussion about gender roles in this country. The media—and the PC police—won't let us.

I'm used to taking rapid fire. On any given day there could be three to four blog posts about something I say on Fox News that triggers hundreds of nasty tweets, emails, and comments. Most people wouldn't get out of bed in the morning if they had my social media accounts. My skin is like an alligator's, and I'll never be bullied into apologizing for what I believe. And I genuinely believe some traditional advice is slowly making a comeback, because all the other crap we've been fed since the rise of feminism has failed us. Women—and men—are desperate for answers.

Sadly, *Glamour* was not as courageous. The backlash was so severe that the magazine felt the need to apologize. Without a hint of irony, the magazine said, "We've been taking some heat for a post on man-pleasing tips that ran here a few days ago—and honestly, we kinda asked for it." That's right—they were asking for it. What an *interesting* choice of words.

It was disappointing. For decades I'd been an avid reader of *Glamour*, even attending their Women of the Year Awards multiple times. Rather than stand by what they printed and leave it up for the sake of a national dialogue or offer an additional defense of what they published by the editor—or even a point/counterpoint by two writers to follow up and encourage more debate—they took the piece down completely, a full redacting.

What so horrified the feminist crowd was that *Glamour* actually tried to recommend ways to keep your man happy instead of making his life miserable (i.e., pretty much every feminist's goal). Their response was "What about the women? What about the women?" The fact that *Glamour* is a women's magazine, and that articles about pleasing women might be more appropriate to *GQ* and *Esquire*, was entirely lost on the outrage machine. To feminists, everything everywhere exists solely to serve whatever their own selfish feelings happen to be.

As I see it, male unhappiness is a problem—and so is female unhappiness. In fact, since we've made this power trade, it is women who are disproportionately more unhappy than men. Even the ultraliberal British newspaper the *Guardian* had an op-ed that asked, *Why are women so "unhappy"?* Desperate to protect her ideology, the author explicitly says, "The more important question to ask ourselves isn't 'Why aren't women happy after

feminism?' It is 'Who cares?'—'happiness' isn't the goal of feminism." No wonder contemporary feminism is so confused and
broken.

All this is hardly a coincidence. Men were less happy when
they had all the power. Now that it's shifted and women have
adopted the traits of men—the incomes, the careers, the respon-
sibilities—*of course* women are going to be saddled with the same
knots that the men had *and* the knots we've had for centuries by
just being women.

For feminists, every problem is a nail and they have the sole
hammer. It's men's fault, it's the patriarchy, we're oppressed. It's
like those quacks who think vitamin C cures scurvy and also
cancer. Yet the feminist argument doesn't match the data. Sexism has decreased in America by every possible measure as female unhappiness has increased. It's not sexism that's causing
this despair to grow—and even if sexism were the main compo-
nent, there are obviously some other factors involved.

There are figures in the culture who are trying to take a whack
at increasing female happiness. Once again, it is Patti Stanger and
Steve Harvey who really get it. Stanger's goal is to get women
into committed monogamous relationships. She understands
that's what most women want. Steve Harvey has advice similar
to the *Glamour* article. He urges women to make sure there are
things that we can do for our men. He insists that men are very
simple, and that there are only three things that a woman needs
to do to keep her man happy: support him; be loyal to him; and
give him the cookie. Harvey is hardly some sort of right-wing
loon, yet he's a cultural phenomenon in part due to his clear-cut
views on relationships.

Harvey's and Stanger's ideas aren't particularly ingenious or
original. Their theories aren't new. In fact that's the whole point:

they're *traditional* theories. Yet there's a reason why the two of them espouse such ideas—and why their books are selling out at bookstores. It's because they have the guts to say out loud what no one else will say. Certainly the knives are out already in the political realm, so any such advice coming from conservatives would be immediately mocked.

Conservatives usually don't want to wade into these issues in any depth—and typically misfire when they do. Rush Limbaugh called activist Sandra Fluke a slut for wanting (free) birth control pills for her friends. (How is having protection indicative of being promiscuous?) Senate candidate Todd Akin's musings about "legitimate rape" will go down in history for their absurdity. And though I like Red State founder Erick Erickson, his claim that the male typically has the "dominant role" when it comes to other species sounds absurd and is simply untrue.

As a result, this type of return-to-tradition advice has permeated the culture without actually being identified for what it is. The media is so averse to conservative ideology that it can't even register it! When Stanger, Harvey, Sandberg, and others advocate traditional, conservative principles, the media conveniently ignores it.

It seems to me that—despite the constant feminist haranguing—many of these pro-women outlets are getting it, very slowly but surely. *Glamour* didn't preemptively self-censor for fear of being called sexist. They didn't see anything wrong with the article at first—their original instincts were the right ones. The article was premised on making your man happy, but there was an implied vice versa. No one is arguing that it shouldn't be a two-way street.

Imagine how insane the feminist overreaction would have sounded if the article had just shifted its subject matter a little bit: "13 Ways to Keep Your Coworker Happy"; "13 Ways to Keep Your Roommate Happy"; "13 Ways to Make Your Kids Happy." None of these would warrant lifting an eyebrow. I'm sure that if *Glamour* ran "13 Ways to Make Your Cat Happy" feminists would share it so much the Internet would implode.

The fact that a woman was being advised to do something nice for a man was somehow a red flag and an encoded message of support for oppression. It's submissive and subservient, and it's beneath us. Number two in that censored article was "Make him a snack after you get it on." What an outrage! I'm guessing feminists treat their cats pretty well, and for them picking up a cat's poop is less demeaning than slapping some cold cuts in between two slices of bread. Feces is empowerment; food is oppression. What a load of BS.

What's the point of being a powerful woman—a powerful human—if you can't use that power to help people you like? And since when does power equal a lack of kindness? If my brother is hungry and I make him a sandwich, am I a "subservient" sister? If my mom is hungry and I *don't* make her a sandwich, what kind of person am I? It's not being subservient; it's being kind and it's being thoughtful.

What, frankly, is the alternative? My man tells me he's hungry and I say, "Too bad, Quiznos is down the street"? That's not the basis for a kind relationship. That's not the basis for *any* kind of relationship. Let's take the stereotypical inverse as a counterexample: "Honey, I really need your help hanging the frame on the wall. I don't know how to do it." How would feminists have the male partner respond? "Screw you, call the handyman"? What if a *GQ* article urged men to give their woman a massage in the shower, as opposed to *Glamour*'s advocating that she hand him a beer? A massage takes far more effort, and yet no one would find that "problematic" at all. In fact, women's outlets praise any kind of editorializing to make women's lives easier. When Sheryl Sandberg wrote in the *New York Times* that men should engage in "choreplay" to help their women around the house, it was almost declared a national holiday.

Personally speaking, if this is a fight the feminists want, if they want to take me on regarding being kind to the people I love, then this is a fight that I'll have all day long—and it's a fight they'll lose. I would like nothing better than to watch them tie themselves up in knots, telling the allegedly heartless conservative to rein in her acts of kindness. Actually, there are some things that I *would* like better, among them being a kind daughter, sister, friend, and girlfriend or wife. Those are things that I endeavor to accomplish as much as possible—as should all women. Houdini demonstrated that the best way to get out of being tied up is to loosen your joints, not stiffen your stance.

The problem is that the feminists' fight isn't just with me. It's with men *and* it's with women, and this is widening the rift between the sexes. Men's magazines haven't yet figured out how to tackle rising female power, though there are columns on how to please a woman; and I'm not speaking of repainting the garage. Being successful in the bedroom entails for most men making sure that the woman has been satisfied (and then some). Guys want to be really good at that and it's something that most men do take pride in. It's one of the few areas where men haven't started going on strike with regard to keeping a woman happy. Whether it's a short-term thing, a long-term thing, or a one-night stand, few guys are indifferent in this department—in part because it's about their reputation and self-image.

Harvey grounds this in men's primal nature. Men want to feel that they can provide and make their woman happy, comfortable, and pleased in the bedroom. It's the perfect complement to the woman being loyal, supportive, and frisky. These are the inherent differences between men and women, but there is a common thread between the genders: it's kindness, respect, and mutual admiration. This thread runs in both directions in a successful relationship, marriage or otherwise.

Women are implicitly being told not to be kind, thoughtful, and nice to the men they love because doing so is supposedly just one step away from being barefoot and pregnant and watching *Leave It to Beaver.* Fine, let's suppose making sandwiches reinforces gender roles. Would fixing his motorcycle be better? If I could do that, I would. Problem is, I can barely figure out my remote controls, let alone how to fix his Harley. "Acts of service" has been a love language—a way to express affection—since time immemorial. Even pets bring food to their owners to show their appreciation.

One relationship I had was with a trial lawyer, which is obviously a very challenging and intense profession. When they're in trial, the attorneys basically go dark for weeks at a time. It's brutal on them. So what did I always do when he was in the thick of it? I stocked his refrigerator with groceries for the week. On Sundays I'd bake him the homemade jalapeño cornbread that he liked along with a giant batch of chili, since I knew that would keep for a few days.

There was nothing political about what I did. I wasn't making some statement. I didn't stand over the stove and recite the Republican Party platform as an incantation to imbue the chili with the full, rich flavor of patriarchal oppression. My motivation was simple: *I didn't want him to worry about anything other than winning his case.* I didn't want him ever thinking, *I'm hungry, I need to order food. What should I get?* I wanted him to be taken care of, so that he could come home, eat something that he enjoyed, take a nap—and then work through the night. I wanted him to be able to focus as much as possible as he prepared for the next day.

In turn he told me that he'd never felt more supported. "I feel your love," he texted me when he'd find the surprise in his refrigerator. This wasn't because I'm some great, amazing cook. It wasn't because I'm a woman. It's because I went out of my way to make his life a little easier, and because I cared. A feminist colleague of mine was horrified when she found out that I was cooking my guy chili. "Why would you do that?" she asked me. "You don't have time to do something like that!"

"You're right," I said, "I really don't have much time to spare. But I want to make time for the people that I value, so I make time on Sundays."

"I just don't get it."

To her it sounded disempowering for a woman like me to assume the role of Betty Crocker. But that was precisely my point: Betty Crocker was a role that I was assuming. I was still a hard-charging conservative television host during the day. If I don't care for the people I love, then who am I caring for? Just myself? That seems a little vain, and selfish. So I don't know which is crazier: that some women hear about my cooking and think of it as subordination, or that some hear me talk about what I did and think of it as boasting. It's neither. It's normal—or at least, in my view, it should be.

The very same women who generally regard me as a throat-slitting right-wing witch also view me as some sort of weak, cowardly shrinking violet in this context. Those are two completely contradictory profiles. Clearly, the feminist critique bears reexamining in this case, because something's not adding up in that analysis.

Of course, kindness needs to go both ways. I currently have a man who is a caring partner in every sense of the word. He is generous and thoughtful and he relishes taking care of me and doing things that help make my life easier. From ordering me new phone chargers so my phone will never die, to ordering dinner for me when I'm up late writing, he is constantly demonstrating his love through his acts of kindness. I'm sure some men would balk at these tasks or think they are beneath them. So what's the difference between him making me a snack and me bringing him a pale ale or making him a grilled cheese?

Quite candidly I am the furthest thing from a 1950s housewife. It's a struggle to find a sharp knife or anything to eat in my kitchen. It's mostly champagne and condiments like hot sauce. If I ask my guy if he's hungry, chances are I'll be ordering him food on Seamless and not whipping up a seven-course meal. So to put me in the same boat as say, Dr. Laura, is quite the stretch.

When I look back, almost every male partner I've chosen has been incredibly kind and has either done more for me than I've done for them or it's been fifty-fifty. Sam would go get me lattes and every gossip magazine on Saturday mornings so I wouldn't have to get out of bed. Others would make me eggs in the morning and bring me my coffee.

The love of my life now is better than any man I have ever met. He is insistent on making sure I'm happy. He ensures I'm not stressed about work, and always offers good advice, stepping in to help and support me in a way that I have never been before. He is a true partner in every sense of the word. I have his back and he has mine. The mutual appreciation and kindness sets the tone for a loving relationship firmly based on equality and mutual respect. Trust me, it works.

But instead of letting men take care of us and advocating for sincere acts of kindness on both sides, women are telling other women to do the opposite. If that *Glamour* column was so wrong, then I have to ask: what do these feminists think is the way to get a man to like you, besides being good at certain sex acts? How *should* women get men to fall for them? What's the new list?

"Don't make a sandwich"? *"Don't* get his favorite drinks"? *"Don't* talk about his childhood"? *"Don't* be nice to his friends"? *Glamour* hasn't published an updated column, so I guess silence in this case is very loud. The new list implicitly is "you shouldn't have to do anything." It's a blank page. Good luck with that, ladies.

That's when we've really become lost as a culture, in my view. *Glamour* retracting its column because of outrage is an example of exactly why women are so messed up. Rather than being fed sandwiches, women are being fed a bowlful of nonsense. We are being pressured to go against our natural urge to do kind, nice things that we may happen to be good at. They may claim otherwise, but here we see exposed the essential message of feminists: *It's always about them.*

The outrage and resulting retraction also point to why *men* are so miserable. These feminists don't give a damn what men think and feel. Whether the guy is hungry, thirsty, needy, or horny, they don't care; it's all about how *they* feel. If everybody is self-involved in their own happiness, then everyone is going to be unhappy because no one is going to be doing nice things for anyone. Though feminists are the ones chiming in about equality in relationships, claiming that they want them to be a two-way street, their actions say otherwise. What they're actually arguing for is a one-way street, which only leads to a romantic cul-de-sac.

Feminism has empowered women to be nasty and aggressive, but has yet to offer an explanation as to why men should celebrate or even *tolerate* such treatment. Feminists like to encourage women to speak out by screaming that "silence is consent" (except in the bedroom, where it's the complete opposite). They've taken the fact that men are choosing not to argue with them as evidence of agreement. But instead, it's evidence of men's increasing frustration, of a sense that there's no upside to arguing with the modern woman, only an enormous downside.

Monogamy does not come easy for men. What's in it for them? Where's the reward? There's no support at home for many modern men. They feel ignored, used, taken for granted, and unappreciated. What man aspires to that?

Men have figured out that unless they actually want to parent full-time, they don't need the opposite sex, either. They can outsource everything that women were traditionally responsible for, from cleaning out their closets to cleaning out their pipes. (Yet they don't have to have their wallets cleaned out in the process.) Who needs a woman to make a home-cooked meal when you can order takeout? Men can send out their laundry and have it delivered. Automatic bill pay takes care of a woman managing the family finances. FreshDirect takes care of grocery shopping.

When men get horny, there are *plenty* of options: Match.com, Internet porn, or a local massage shop that specializes in one specific massage. Our culture has done such a good job of convincing women to view sex like men do that the men can benefit from a booty call without having to buy a woman dinner or even have a basic conversation. We all know *LOL* and *OMG*, but the Internet even has an acronym for this phenomenon, *NSA* sex, meaning no strings attached.

Why buy the cow? Heck, why take any responsibility when it comes to the cow? Men just want to stand near the cow when it's convenient in the hope of some free milk. Lucky for them the pastures are full of calves who give up their milkshakes in the hopes they bring all the boys to the yard. It used to be that women would set high expectations for men, and men would strive to meet them. Now both sexes are failing each other.

Matriarch of the Kardashian family and legendary momager Kris Jenner already had four young kids when she went on a blind date with Bruce Jenner in 1990. Bruce had his own children from a previous marriage. He didn't need to take on a woman with four pieces of baggage. He could have married anyone but *chose* to raise Kris's son and three daughters as his own. This was a noble act that demonstrates how reliable and goodhearted he is as a person. Yet despite his sacrifice, despite his character, despite his accomplishments, Jenner rarely got the respect he deserved from his family.

Kris Jenner used her bravado and her bullish, controlling ways to turn her daughters into stars and her household into the Kardashian empire. The cameras captured a marriage that was always all about Kris. Lots of laughs were had on the show over Jenner being the last to know important information, as when Khloe decided to marry NBA star Lamar Odom after knowing him only a few weeks. The Kardashian family centered an entire episode on keeping Jenner in the dark about this revelation. While Bruce shuffled around the house like an outcast, the Kardashian women howled at how hysterical it was that he was out of the loop. The cameras followed Bruce's ignorance to the whole issue—and then documented his hurt feelings after learning that he had been the last to know. Where Bethenny Frankel was known to verbally castrate her husband, in his television career Bruce Jenner went from former Olympian to household joke to woman. It took putting on a dress and transitioning for Caitlyn to get treated with respect from her family.

In an interview during Jenner's transition period Kris blamed herself for the sex change. "Kris has tried to say this is all her fault," reported the Hollywood Gossip. Kris believed that Bruce's transition to Caitlyn reflected poorly on her as a wife. And during Caitlyn's famous sit-down with Diane Sawyer she said she was cast as the family's "punching bag." Bruce's transition from man to woman obviously wasn't caused by Kris's domineering ways, but it illustrates a critical point in the way women are acting toward guys: *we are acting like the men.*

It was impossible to watch even a single episode of *Keeping Up with the Kardashians* without getting a feel for how horrible life was for Bruce under that roof. Every choice he made was both criticized and controlled. He even moved into the garage for a while so he wouldn't have to face his family's scrutiny and ridicule—especially from his wife. Of course such mistreatment didn't make him decide to transition, but it certainly didn't help his process or make living life as a man easy. It was much more natural for Bruce to exist in that family as a woman. That's the problem with America: men are often the forgotten figure of the home.

My mom always said that steel sharpens steel, meaning that couples are better as a team. Women should *want* to help their man succeed and do well. The better he does at work, the better she'll do—and vice versa. As I said, that team concept was pushed very heavily by Sheryl Sandberg and her late husband, Dave Goldberg, and both deserve a lot of credit for their stance. When he passed away, all of America should have been mourning the loss of a very confident man, a real role model for husbands to look up to.

Dave Goldberg was the CEO of SurveyMonkey, but he is far more commonly remembered as "Sheryl Sandberg's husband." Goldberg was a man who was married to a powerful woman and wasn't intimidated by her. He celebrated her strength, built her up, and was a true partner to her. His final goal had been to encourage men to lean in to help their women. His sudden death in 2015 somewhat put the brakes on what was starting to become a real cultural conversation. The two of them were the first couple to get the Facebook and broader social media crowd to take a look at the same arguments that I'm making. But these ideas are not the dominant ones in our feminized culture. Feminists are determined to keep women unhappy. If we were all happy, they'd have nothing to write about. On *Outnumbered*, we recently debated an article by a woman who ranted about how upsetting it was to her that she hadn't used a hammer in ages. Her husband was so helpful that she didn't have to, and thus lost a sense of herself. Talk about a first-world problem. There are millions of women who would kill to find a husband who likes to lean in with his tool kit. Many of these women are single moms.

I would have loved to see Goldberg pen an article about being married to a very smart, successful, ambitious ass-kicker—who also happened to be an amazing wife. It would have been fascinating to see how he as a man handled that, especially without losing his masculinity in the process. But instead their most prominent piece on the issue was an *Esquire* essay by *her*, with asides from him inserted throughout. Why was Sheryl Sandberg in a men's magazine, telling men how to be? Such insights are constant and pervasive. His perspective is not—and now can never be. So here's mine:

TEN WAYS TO HANDLE A POWERFUL FEMALE PARTNER

by Andrea Tantaros

1. Be persistent.
2. Don't patronize her.
3. Give her space.
4. Love her wild side.
5. Don't try to tame her; just admire her.
6. Treat her like an equal.
7. Savor her strength.

8. Match her fire with yours.
9. If you can't handle the heat, move it along.
10. Buckle up!

In 2010 Jennifer Aniston starred in a romcom called *The Switch*. "Women are realizing more and more that you don't have to settle, they don't have to fiddle with a man to have that child," she said at the time. "They're realizing if it's that time in their life and they want this part, they can do it with or without *that*." ("That" here refers to a man, and is the most objectifying term possible.)

Let's discuss what women are actually "doing without" when they opt to go it alone. We're talking money, we're talking support in every sense of the word, and we're talking additional love for the child. No matter what your gender may be, single parenting is a serious undertaking even with a huge bankroll and around-the-clock assistance. Being a single parent is one of the hardest jobs in the world. They deserve major credit.

Though Aniston may be Greek like me, she and I had very different childhoods. She grew up as the daughter of a famous soap opera actor. I'm the daughter of a poor immigrant who made it rich, one who practically raised me in our family restaurant. Many of the waitresses who worked there were single moms. There was nothing glamorous for them about raising kids alone. These weren't the actions of women who had been "liberated" from men. They didn't aspire to be Murphy Brown. I remember more than one time when a waitress couldn't find a sitter and brought her child to the restaurant. I'd watch that kid get put in a back booth to color while the mom worked her shift.

While people have discussed the effects of single motherhood on the mothers themselves and on their children, what many people don't realize is how much this message affects another group: men. Telling men they aren't needed has had dangerous social repercussions. As John Gray wrote in *Men Are from Mars, Women Are from Venus*, "Not to be needed is a slow death for a man. When a man doesn't feel he is making a positive difference in someone else's life, it is hard for him to continue caring about his life and his relationships. It is difficult to be motivated when he is not needed."

Director Judd Apatow has showcased just how pathetic modern men are viewed in films like *This Is Forty*. Paul Rudd is a father, a husband, and a doormat. He's disrespected by his wife in front of their children. She has no issue lobbing swearwords at him and calling him a loser. The kids, in turn, tell their father to F off as easily as they say good morning. What's meant to be funny ends up being really troubling to watch. In the film, Rudd would rather masturbate while sitting on the toilet than have sex with his wife. Why any man—or any *human*—would want to sleep with someone constantly cursing at them must escape the writers. Here's the thing: *they don't*.

What's happening as a result of this is that the men are fighting back . . . quietly. It starts early. In late 2015, author Jonathan Haidt discussed a visit he had made to a high school class. The students universally agreed that they wanted to hear both sides of every issue. Haidt asked the female students if they felt like they had to walk on eggshells. One or two raised their hands. But when he asked the boys, almost all of them did. We're not seeing a war against women. We're seeing a *surrender* against us. It's manifesting itself—this concept of men fighting back—in how they treat us, especially sexually and romantically.

Men are increasingly choosing not to get married, and I can see why. One of my guy friends put it very well. In his view—and I agree—men are deeply fearful that women will do whatever it takes to get a man to the altar. They will be kind; they will show that they can do bedroom gymnastics and all these other things; they may even slap together the dreaded bologna sandwich of oppression.

However, that all comes to a screeching halt on the wedding day. Then it just shuts down and becomes all about the wife and not the husband. He's an appendage to her and the life that she wants to lead. As a successful woman, there are times I've been somewhat ambivalent about getting married myself. I even asked myself the obvious question: would I be more interested in marriage if I were a man, or less?

It took about one second to figure out the answer.

Nowadays, women withhold all the love languages. They're too busy to offer quality time and uninterested in offering words of affirmation. Giving gifts? Acts of service? Oh no, that's beneath the modern woman. And there's the old standby: the withholding of sex, and the intimacy and pleasure that it entails. The icing on this twisted cake is that they're also needy. Selfish *and* needy? There's a losing combo if I've ever heard one.

It's one thing if you're going to be needy but you're also making the guy a sandwich, bringing him beers, and are all over him. Some men would tolerate that. I'm sure it can get annoying after a while, but there's really no relationship where *something* isn't annoying to each partner. At the very least, in this scenario the man feels supported and appreciated. He feels needed, because he actually *is*. If women are to be intellectually honest, then we must start admitting that we do need men. Not for everything, but there are certain voids that female friends and being alone cannot fill.

But women today aren't giving. Logically, the guys are asking themselves what's in it for them. Why would they walk down the aisle and sign up for that? No matter which way you slice it, the man isn't getting much out of the exchange. It's a bad deal. Worse, if he decides to bail on the unhappy situation, he has to give her half his money. He's effectively paying someone in perpetuity for the privilege of being her servant, handyman, and psychologist.

The divorce laws in this country are insane and outdated—but barely ever register a peep from feminists. They're more interested in the gender wage gap than in touching laws that so disproportionately benefit women. Again, it's not about equality whatsoever. It's all about power and control, even if they won't admit this to themselves. Their uncharacteristic silence on this topic speaks volumes.

Liberals seem unable or unwilling to accept the fact that people respond to economic incentives. If your unemployment check is equivalent to your former salary, there is no reason to work other than some vague notion of fairness. Some on the left concede this point and realize that marginal increases in handouts result in marginal decreases in the workforce. They counter by pointing out that even though some people are going to game the system, we still need to have a safety net in place to catch the vast bulk of those suffering from, say, a systemic downturn.

That's not an unfair position to take. Does everyone want to be on unemployment for the rest of their lives? Of course not. Many wealthy people who don't need to work choose to work anyway, and for myriad reasons. Similarly, some people simply don't want to work no matter what the circumstances. The vast majority fall somewhere in between. The larger point here is this: The more successful the man is, the more likely he is to look at the economic consequences of any life decisions that he makes. It doesn't take a forensic accountant to see that there's a huge financial disincentive for successful men to get married in our country.

The older you get, the more divorced couples you know—and the more horror stories you hear. In New York State, a medical license is regarded as marital property. Yes, both halves of a married couple have equal claim to the doctor's license to practice medicine. When the divorce happens, the court figures out how much the doctor is expected to earn for the rest of his life. Then the other partner gets half of that. Since male doctors outnumber female doctors two-to-one in New York, the outcome is skewed heavily in one direction. Odd that the true-blue home state of "feminist" senator Hillary Clinton did nothing to address this concern.

Yet even that's not so bad, since no doctor will ever be out of a job. Men are overwhelmingly less risk-averse than women, so they are far more represented in industries with unsteady incomes. I knew a man who was making half a million dollars a year working in finance. Like so many others, he got laid off during the 2008 meltdown. His wife filed the divorce papers immediately after he lost his job, demonstrating once again the limitless cruelty that women are capable of.

The courts viewed his most recent $500,000 income as his earning potential, and ordered this unemployed man to pay his ex-wife the commensurate amount of alimony. This newly divorced guy didn't have any income to provide for himself, let alone his family. He of course couldn't make his payments, and got thrown in jail as a consequence of laws ostensibly designed to fight deadbeat dads and ex-husbands.

It's *impossible* to imagine this situation in reverse, with an ex-wife being thrown in jail under these circumstances. Feminists have done a really good job at leveling the playing field in the courts with much-needed legislation against rape and crimes against women. But it is absurdly obvious that the courts are tilted in favor of women in cases of divorce. This is one of the lowest-hanging fruit in terms of fighting gender inequality, and yet somehow it seems to be the one thing that feminists aren't outraged about.

Of course, there are notable exceptions where the woman was overwhelmingly the breadwinner and paid. Roseanne Barr's divorce from Tom Arnold was probably the first major such case, and more recently the story repeated with Jessica Simpson and Nick Lachey. Women increasingly have the earning potential and the power, but our divorce laws are based on the premise that a woman can't be expected to provide for herself for the rest of her life. In actual fact, it's the men who are finding themselves in shambles after the marriage ends. "Ball and chain" has gone from referring to the wife to describing the alimony payments that ex-husbands are paying out for years.

Guys are running around retelling these stories at the gym, at bars, and at work. They feel—correctly—that their first marriage wrecked their life. They resent that their ex-wives are feeding off their money while they're having trouble restarting their lives again, especially in a financial sense. This is even more the case when men have careers with a finite span, like athletes. The glory days end but the alimony payments don't. It's no surprise that women fantasize about marriage but men are terrified of divorce.

I have actually lived this dilemma myself. While I agree with Sheryl Sandberg that having the right partner is of utmost importance, unfortunately it feels like the "right partner" might have to be the right divorce attorney if things go south in an eventual marriage. If I choose the wrong guy, my husband would end up taking a huge chunk of everything that I've worked for—and as a woman in television, I don't think I'm going to be sitting on the end of the couch in the "leg chair" at seventy years old. Why embark on a marriage if it just becomes inevitable bankruptcy, or misery? That's why Sheryl Sandberg's point about picking the right partner is so paramount.

Women are only getting more successful. We're both going to have to handle that but men don't have to be intimidated by it. Sure, we're wired differently. We need to understand that we have different dreams and goals, different primal instincts. But thoughtfulness, understanding, and mutual respect are key. Everyone loves to be valued and respected. As long as that's maintained—and it's not completely unbalanced—the partnership can thrive. The inverse is true as well: no unbalanced relationship is going to work, whether it's a friendship or more.

If the culture really started to embrace such a message, I think we would see at the very least an increase in committed relationships.

The problem is, we have to act fast, as I discovered after my breakup. The culture is changing right before our eyes. It's mindboggling but most twenty-something women have never been on a formal date (that is, dinner and some kind of activity, instead of just coming over for a Budweiser and a BJ). Men don't do it because women don't demand it. Women are giving men oral sex after a few beers—and then wondering why the man doesn't act like Prince Charming after the act. More and more men and women are "ghosting" each other when they don't want to see the other person. You used to give the guy or gal a face-to-face meeting, or at least a phone call. Now people vanish into thin air without any explanation. It isn't just hurtful; it's hurtful *and* rude.

To turn the hippie quote around, suppose they gave a war and everyone came—and then put on their clothes and went home, never speaking to one another again? There's not a war on men or, again, a war on women. *There's a war on kindness, manners, politeness, and courtesy. There's a war on commitment and monogamy.* Those aren't the explicit targets, but they're the casualties nevertheless. And since the two sides in the conflict—men and women—aren't even communicating with one another, since technology makes it easy to ignore each other, we ignore the problems, too.

Any attempt to engage in a conversation brings forth outrage and silencing. Many women don't want to deal with Sandwichgate and will be intimidated into shutting up. So much for women being able to speak their minds and choose. As a result, *no one is even acknowledging what's happening.* If you can't negotiate, you can't negotiate a cease-fire—let alone a truce—and the war between the sexes simply goes on in perpetuity. This isn't progress.

Part II

The Unmaking
of Americans

Chapter 6

Webs of Emotion

I T'S NO SECRET that my reputation is that of a combative conservative. My mom says that I honed my toughness and my debate skills on her when I was a teenager: "Why can't I go out longer?" "Why can't I date?" "Why can't I get my ears double pierced?" She's pretty psyched the liberals have to deal with me now. While there's an element of truth to her version of events—my poor parents!—I think that my fighting spirit was actually developed at a far younger age.

One time when I was a teenager, my mom got me to take a few college aptitude tests to gauge what my strengths were. I was terrible at math and science and ~~real~~ very good at English and writing—but my social justice score, the measure of moral reasoning, was through the roof. I guess you could say Andrea Tantaros was a natural-born social justice warrior.

I really was a "warrior" for as long as I can remember. That's because I wasn't fighting for myself, but for my younger brother, Dan. I'm the third Tantaros kid. To Dean and Thea, I'm the little sister. But Dean and Thea are twelve and ten years older than me, respectively. Even though they were our big siblings, they essentially grew up in a different era. It was Dan and I who grew up together. Dan was the youngest, three years behind me, so I was a big sister to him and only him. I undertook that role with all the fiery intensity that one might expect.

Dan had been born with the umbilical cord wrapped around his neck. My mom knew something was wrong from the moment she saw the look on the doctor's face. She had seen the physician's expression when her other three children were born. This time his face was sheer panic: Dan was blue. Only a few weeks later Dan had to undergo two surgeries. The first was to correct his vision so that his eyes wouldn't cross. The second was to ensure that the plates in his tiny cranium didn't fuse, so that his brain could grow properly.

After he left Philadelphia's Children's Hospital, my parents were hopeful that all would be okay. But in the following months my mom recognized that Dan wasn't making eye contact. He didn't laugh as much as Dean, Thea, and I had, and he rarely engaged in purposeful play. A few visits to a neurologist gave us the diagnosis: autism. That made growing up a very different experience both for Dan and for us siblings.

Dan didn't stand out as much as a child as he would when he got older. But we all know that kids hone in on the slightest differences, and there was no hiding that Dan wasn't like the other kids in the neighborhood. He didn't talk and he drooled a little bit. Whenever he went out in public the other kids would stare at him. Sometimes they would point. I'd hear them ask their parents the same questions: "Why is that kid wearing a bib?" "Why is he making those noises?" "Why is he drinking the water in the swimming pool?" "What's wrong with him?" Let me answer that last one: *there was absolutely nothing wrong with my brother.* At the time these children were known as handicapped. But today I think it's the rest of the world that's not normal. People with disabilities have their priorities and are much better positioned than the rest of us, who, let's face it, can be pretty screwed up at times.

I was always acutely in tune with what was going on around me, especially when I was with Dan. Whenever I picked up on kids making fun of Dan or even just gesturing at him, my mind had only one thought: *protect*. And when my mind is in protect mode, that means that my mouth is in attack mode. I might come off as scary now, but even I wouldn't want to cross little Andrea.

First they'd get the glare if they looked at Dan for too long. Then I'd just snap at them: "What are *you* lookin' at?" It got so bad that even my mom told me to rein it in. "Andrea," she said time and again, "you can't go around constantly making faces at other kids or fighting back in Dan's defense." Over the years virtually everything my mom taught me turned out to be true. I suspect that in this case she was right, too, that if I had just changed my tone then maybe I could have had some better outcomes.

Yet I never really took my mom's advice in this instance. Who else was going to protect Dan? I was the big sister, and that's *my* duty and *my* mission—and I was proud to do it. I never showed emotion about Dan in public. I never showed embarrassment over Dan. I never cried about the way that my brother was. I never wished he was "normal." I would never wish that I had a brother who was different than Dan. I was never ashamed of him, ever. There were never tears over Dan, only feelings of love—and of guilt.

When we were little, a friend of our parents once said, "When Andrea was born she took everything—all the good genes—and left nothing for Dan." I didn't realize at the time how insidious that comment was, and how much it would come to affect my perspective. I wasn't the one who had any seizures. I wasn't the one who had to wear those conspicuous helmets. Dan really shouldn't have had a reason to want to get out of bed in the morning, but he never complained. He couldn't. I had to be that proverbial voice for the voiceless. Everything he did was hard, and I was going to do everything I could to make it easier for him.

It's Dan who is most responsible for conditioning me to be a fighter.

As Dan got older he was frequently in and out of the hospital. A couple of times he almost died, and yet I still never showed emotion about it. It was only when he passed away in August 2013 that I lost it. Here's where things got tricky. When you're on television and somewhat of a public figure, it's not always possible to grieve in private.

The day after Dan's passing, a cohost offered to make the announcement on *The Five*. For a moment during the mourning period I felt a sense of relief, because that meant that maybe I wouldn't have to talk about it myself.

Obviously I've had spontaneous moments of emotion that I couldn't control at different times. After ten years of gymnastics and twelve of dance competitions I was conditioned to not get scared in front of a crowd. But never had I been faced with the fact that I might have to be emotional on national television—and if I was talking about Dan's passing, there was no way I could be emotionless.

They say there's no crying in baseball. Well, there also isn't any real crying in television either, or at least in the news business. It's very rare that you see people shedding a tear while doing reporting or analysis. The Kennedy assassination, the 9/11 attacks—the reporters act as cool as cucumbers while inside they're experiencing the exact same emotions as everyone else.

One of the reasons we still remember the *Hindenburg* disaster is because that reporter lost his composure. That's how rare it is for a journalist to lose it.

When I returned to *The Five*—and I returned very quickly—I knew that there would be questions. I knew that I might have to address Dan's passing on the show myself. The cards and letters kept pouring in based on the announcement. I think the only person who got more letters than me that year was Santa Claus—and all he got were demands. All I got was love and support and caring from complete strangers who for whatever reason happen to like watching me on television.

I would sit in my office day after day and read the heartfelt notes from viewers as tears streamed down my face. I would read words of comfort from people I had never met, prayer cards, stories about how they, too, had understood loss, or about how they had a special needs sibling. I was touched and downright overwhelmed at how caring the Fox audience was for someone whom most of them had never even met.

Naturally *The Five*'s producers thought that I needed to say something myself. The viewers wanted to know if I was okay, and the staff felt that I should honor my brother on the show. At first I didn't know if I wanted to. When my father passed away five years before, I was only a Fox contributor. I didn't have a show or a devoted audience who took the time to spend sixty minutes of their precious day with me. Now I was a daily presence in people's homes and expectations were different. I understood where the producers were coming from, and logically I could see that they were right. Still, it felt like I would be exposing a part of myself that I just wasn't really comfortable with. It would mean sharing with the entire audience that I'm not as tough as I come across.

What people might not realize about Fox is that the network always encourages us to be who we want to be. I can't think of another network that would allow me to truly be who I am—and at that point in time I was a human being who was hurting.

I owed a large part of my success on *The Five* to Dan. I don't just mean his crucial role in developing my strong personality. When the show first launched, I asked my boss for any advice. "Be yourself," he said. "Roger Ailes sees something in you and your background, and he wants that to come across on-screen. Talk about your family. Talk about growing up in the restaurant. Be authentic."

I tried to follow that advice, but during my first five years at the network I was on one speed: attack the liberals. As a young girl in her twenties I felt like I had to prove myself on TV by being aggressive and sharp, rather than letting loose and having fun or interjecting things from my personal life. I wasn't always comfortable talking about working in my father's diner. Talking about myself felt like being egotistical. "Let others' lips praise you," my mom had drilled in my head when I was younger.

When I had to get personal, it was Dan whom I leaned on. I was comfortable talking about our relationship growing up, and telling all those funny stories about what it was like having a special needs brother. I knew I could always discuss Dan because there was something so endearing about him. So if I was to be true to myself—and to the audience that had been so supportive—then I would have to say something about his passing on the air.

I just didn't know if I could.

For me to talk about what Dan meant—knowing that he was gone and never coming back—was a whole different challenge. Did I *really* want to go there and show the audience what our relationship was like, knowing that there was a very good chance that I couldn't hold it together? If lost it in front of the cameras, it wouldn't just be shedding a tear. If I lost it on the air, I knew that it would be a full-on breakdown on live television.

I went into my office and tried to practice, but I just couldn't get through what I wanted to say. I kept sobbing and even when I could sense that I was about to start crying there was nothing I could do about it. I began to have second thoughts and called my producer, Susan Wertheim. I tried brainstorming ways to get out of what I needed to do: Should I have someone else do it? Should I shorten what I wanted to say? Maybe I could just acknowledge Dan's passing and move on, thanking the viewers for all their cards but then quickly changing the subject.

Susan listened politely and then put a stop to it. "Andrea, you can do this," she said.

It took me six attempts before I felt comfortable enough to go on-air and say what I needed to. I went to get my hair done and my makeup *re*done. As showtime got closer and closer I grew increasingly nervous. Thankfully my makeup artist knew what to say to keep me going. "Don't you dare cry!" she told me. "If you ruin my perfect makeup, I'll kill you!"

It was one thing to memorialize Dan in the privacy of my office. It was a whole other thing to do it in front of cameras and under stage lights. When it was my turn to do the "One More Thing" segment I looked down and took a deep breath. As I began to speak I started to well up. I could sense my voice starting to crack and I knew what was going to come next. *You can't totally lose it*, I told myself, *because then no one is listening to you. Then they won't even be able to understand you. That's not doing Dan any justice.*

I got my voice together and continued, only pausing to allow

my chin to get that one quiver in. I closed by quoting an email
from a fan from Encinitas, California, named Steve, who had a
special needs son of his own: "The level of love you allow yourself
to reach for a person of unfathomable innocence is far beyond
any love that most people will ever know in their lives. That is
their greatest gift." It was so true. In his entire life, Dan never
said a negative word about anybody. In his entire life, he never
hurt anyone's feelings. I can't say that about anyone else I know.
He was so sinless that he softened our entire family and taught
us how to love big. Having him as my brother was a pure, undi-
luted blessing. He reprioritized my life and the lives of everyone
in our family.

Then, it was over. I had managed to get through what I
needed to say in one go. It was the most choked up I've ever been
on national television, and it was the most authentic. I *chose* to
show emotion and I'm glad that I did. As intense as the experience was, my little monologue on *The Five* about Dan was also
very freeing. Choking up on the air let everybody know that I do
have tear ducts. ("So the Republican does have a heart?" is a line
I've heard before.) Since then I've grown a bit more comfortable
professionally with cracking when topics get tough.

Because I'm so much on one side of politics, I kept thinking
that I couldn't let the liberals see me in a weakened state. I didn't
want my enemies to have footage of me crying. I had a reputation
to uphold, right? In retrospect any fears I had were completely
misguided. Somehow I had equated my tears with being weak.
In actuality, I think that it's pretty frigging strong to be able to
drop your guard. Look at a literal fight. It is the weak person who
assumes the defensive position, not the strong one. The strong
one allows themselves to be exposed, because they know they
have the strength to take that hit if necessary.

As great as the fan response was when the initial announcement was made, the response after I said my piece was even stronger. People *want* authenticity. They're sick of phonies. We might admire people for their strength, but we relate to them for their passion. We're tired of displays of emojis in lieu of emotions.

Given how positive the response was and how liberating it felt, I started to ask the obvious question: Why is there any pressure against crying to begin with? Looking back on my own life, I remember not having an issue with it in junior high. Nor was it an issue in high school or even college. It was when I went into politics after college that it sort of hit. I was now in a man's environment, and I was expected to buck up. You don't cry in the office—in *any* office. This was certainly the case when I worked in Washington, D.C., and in the rough-and-tumble world of political campaigns. There the men will look at you like you're a lunatic if you get emotional about anything.

For me, one of the best expositions of women and their challenges with crying came from an episode of *Sex and the City*, the series that was a cultural touchstone for so many. On the show, the Samantha character is a sort of masculine alpha type who beds a different man every night with zero attachment. Of the four main characters she's the closest thing to a guy. I suspect that the only reason she was written onto the show was to get men to watch. While everyone knows some promiscuous woman, rarely do such women fail to express any emotion. They never spend their entire lives shirking any kind of relationship, marriage, kids, or true intimacy with the opposite sex. It's just not realistic.

This particular episode had Samantha trying to secure a position with a hotel magnate. He explicitly tells her that he doesn't want to hire her because he wants the job to go to another guy. Frustrated, Samantha pushes him on that point. She insists that she is equipped to do the work. Finally, the magnate relents a bit and suggests that she share the work with a man. Samantha is confused. She believes that she doesn't need to share the work with a man, and tells the magnate as much.

The magnate eventually comes clean to Samantha. The actual reason why he isn't hiring her comes down to one thing: she had slept with one of his architects. She's stunned to have her personal life thrust in front of her like that, especially in a professional setting. Samantha—who never cries on the show—starts to feel herself welling up. She gives the magnate a firm fight before she loses it. She points out that if she had been a man, he would have "slapped her on the ass, handed her a scotch, and given her the keys to the closest corner office." Instead, being a woman, she is only given the door.

Having gotten that off her chest, Samantha runs out of his office before she begins bawling. The magnate chases after her and catches up to her by the elevator. She frantically hits the button so that she can escape with what remains of her dignity intact. She manages to make a clean getaway—and the next day he brings her back to the office to tell her that she got the job because he's never seen someone with "balls as big as hers." As a viewer it was compelling to see an alpha woman show emotion. It was like seeing a dog walk on its hind legs for four hours straight. It was *amazing*. He witnessed her strength, but he never saw her tears. It was a moment that so many women can identify with, but it points to the struggle we still have when it comes to showing emotion.

Sex and the City had a strong reputation because it showcased the many facets of the complicated issues that women face. Another scene in that episode had Charlotte, a more uptight preppy type, lamenting that she was caught crying once at an art gallery.

As a result, she was forevermore branded as the girl who cries—which is exactly what women don't want. We don't want to be that story that guys tell their friends, " . . . and then she started crying." (Eye rolls and groans usually follow.)

While it's usually a sign of authenticity, crying is more widely branded as a sign of instability—and not just a sign, but proof positive. It's all you need to know about a woman before dismissing her entirely. You can't trust anything that comes out of her mouth, and why would you want that toxicity nearby anyway? As one of my guy friends put it, "Women are like cars: they're no good if they keep breaking down." Well, it's not that simple, because the reasons why women cry aren't particularly simple, either.

Throughout my life, there have been women in the workplace who cry a lot—and they're known as crazy crying women. The thing is, some of them legitimately *are* insane. Then there are the ones who sort of just do it. We've even had a few cry on *Outnumbered* simply because something had moved them. In my view, that's not crazy at all. The audience agrees with me. To them, it's gripping and raw. Finally, there are the Samanthas, the ones like a girl I knew who used to go in the bathroom to cry when the boys' club got too difficult to endure. "AT, never let 'em see you sweat," Governor Weld once told me. But I tried to take it even further: never let 'em see you sweat *or* cry.

The expression "damned if you do, damned if you don't" certainly applies to women and our tears. Every woman knows that there's an internal push and pull when it gets to be too much. We regret crying and we regret not crying. We're aware of those forty-eight hours every month where we really could potentially murder someone and should be able to get away with it. Every man who's been in a relationship sure knows about those forty-eight hours, too, when his partner seems to be literally crazy.

Yet it's not just a problem during a certain time of the month. I have resisted showing my feelings with men, and so too does almost every other woman. If you get too emotional, it's a bad thing. We worry that it'll scare them away. Sure, Whitney Houston's song is pretty catchy: "I get so emotional, baby, every time I think of you." It sounds great on the radio but in real life saying that to a man makes a woman sound unhinged.

Women suppress our feelings in order to act more stoic—in other words, to act more like men. We don't want to act on our natural emotions because we don't want the guy to think that we care. If we cry, then he thinks we're really into him and are totally attached. Rather than expressing anything in a healthy way, we simply end up shelving a lot of our thoughts. We act this way while knowing full well how unhealthy it is to repress any emotion for too long.

Why is there such a push to make people less authentic? Why are we trying to be something we're not? In my view, a lot of it is fueled by social media. Sure, you can take a picture and make yourself look thin and tan and strong. But in real life, you can't always look like the photo. You can't always be your Instagram shot doing a handstand or a crow pose or whatever. There has to be a time and a place to let the walls down.

I started dating the love of my life in the fall of 2015. After only a week of dating he caught a segment on *Outnumbered*, where we were discussing whether or not couples should be best friends. Rather than admit that I wanted my husband to be my closest confidant, the person I could tell everything to, I tempered my response to one that was inauthentic—something I never do on television.

"I don't think women should tell their men everything. Leave some mystery. They can't be your best friend." These words came from a place of hurt and a fear of being burned again. These words were not me. I hoped he wouldn't notice.

Later that evening he mentioned the conversation. I tried to justify it by saying that there were going to be things I didn't want him to know. I spun that those things had to do with "feminine issues" like my monthly cycle, bikini waxing, or a bathroom crisis. He wasn't buying it and he never forgot it.

As time passed we became best friends. I trust him implicitly, and as our love grew deeper and we grew closer, I found myself hoping he would never bring up my phony on-air dodge of my true feelings again.

And then one night it hit me: nobody loved me more at that moment than he did, more than any man ever had. It was the most protected and cared for I had ever felt since my father died. I felt the tears welling up but didn't want him to see me cry. The more he looked at me the more I knew I had to be authentic and take down the wall.

"You are my best friend." The tears began to flow.

He smiled. "Those are the best words I could ever hear. But what happened to that girl on TV, the one who said couples can't be best friends?"

"She wasn't being honest."

I let my guard down and showed a side of me that nobody ever sees. I knew that if I wanted him to be vulnerable with me, then it was only fair that I show some vulnerability myself. The same holds true when it comes to letting him in and speaking up for what I want out of our relationship. My dad always pointed out in his Greek accent that, no matter how obvious it might seem to you, people don't know what you're thinking. "Andrea, you've gotta tell people what you want in life. They're not mind readers. What's the worst they're gonna say? 'No'? You're not gonna die."

My father was right. You never die, though rejection can feel like it. If a person cares about you in some fashion, then they will accept your emotions and feel for you. If, on the other hand, they try to make you feel bad for being authentic . . . well, there's really no point in having any meaningful sort of relationship with someone like that. There's no good reason to want someone around you that you can't be yourself with. Eventually, the mask slips and they'll see who you really are. The only real long-term options are either showing them up front, or wasting your time.

Here again is an example of how we women screwed ourselves over by saying that we have to be like men. *We shouldn't have to suppress our own feelings.* If we aren't liberated to be our own selves, then what is the purpose of feminism at all? How did "liberation" become code for "repression"? This observation isn't unique to myself. I know that Jill Abramson talked about this in the context of being fired from the *New York Times.* Yes, we shouldn't be having meltdowns on our boss's desk. But neither should we be hiding all those real emotions—even from the guys we're with.

The double standard between the genders is very profound on this issue. In 2008 the media was obsessed when Hillary Clinton cried one day at a coffee shop in New Hampshire; they credited it for her win in the primary there. "Certainly it was impressive that she could choke up and stay on message," gushed frequent Clinton critic Maureen Dowd of the *New York Times.* On the other hand, former Speaker of the House John Boehner used to cry all the time. Sure, they poked fun at him, but in the long run it never got him the attention that Hillary got. Look how much praise Jimmy Kimmel received when he cried over a lion being shot simply for sport. President Obama has been universally critiqued for his cold aloofness; when he delivered the most important announcement of our generation and his presidency, that thanks to the Navy SEALs of SEAL Team Six Osama bin Laden had been killed, he sounded like a robot. He later tried to make up for it with some very unconvincing tears when he announced his gun control executive action. Contrast that with President George W. Bush. For all the vitriol that was leveled against him, no one thought him weak for shedding a tear when our country was attacked. He would get welled up over some things at the podium, and it endeared him to people on some level. He was pilloried without mercy—but no one called him a sissy. That's progress for the *men*, while the *women* have regressed.

Women put more pressure on ourselves not to cry than is actually required. I get savaged on a daily basis by the loony left. Yet none of those leftists took me to task for losing my composure on the air over my brother's passing. It was probably the one day where I wasn't a clickbait headline for some horrible site. It's okay to show emotion. No one cares, no one judges, if it's *real*. If a woman is faking emotion to keep a guy or to win an election then it's a problem. The problem there is the deception, not the tears per se. When it comes to crying and emotion, we women are our own toughest critics. We think that we have to be like the boys—or worse, like emotionless statues who are above it all. This is exactly the wrong message, and the worst thing is, *we know it*. The most progress I've made in relationships has occurred when I've let down the walls and just been myself. If that means feeling emotion in that moment, then that's fine.

Tears are a release. Even the strongest man in the world has a weight that he simply cannot budge. Being stronger than anyone isn't the same thing as being stronger than anything. Every person on earth has an emotional limit that they can't get past. Showing that you've reached that limit makes people who like you want to help you, rather than condemn you. For women, it's either man up or be perceived as a cuckoo bird. That's not fair, but it's one of the biggest knots that women wrestle with.

It's not just with tears that women are in a bind. I've been a consultant for female political candidates, and in political races the men can get away with things that women never can. A female candidate can look strong or tough or determined—all great things. But she can't look angry. The public will not accept a woman who looks pissed off.

I've spoken to Secret Service agents who worked for Michelle Obama under deep cover. Regardless of their politics, they all agreed that she is quite possibly the kindest and most gracious first lady they've ever worked for. I'm sure the whole "angry black woman" meme didn't help her reputation, but there was one other minor point that hurt her public perception: her eyebrows. It was reported that she had to get a makeover because her brows had been sculpted in a way that was too pointy, and was read as too angry. If anyone doubts the power of eyebrows, think of the emoticons :-) vs. >:-).

Men don't have to worry about their eyebrows. Guys can get away with being pissed off. When men get too intense they look protective and masculine. Women come off as out of control, like they're PMSing to the nth degree. I'm tested regularly when it comes to displaying anger because people on the left often make the argument personal. It's not enough that they think that I'm wrong; I must actually be a horrible person to boot. To be totally fair, there are a number of Democrats whom I debate who are wonderful. People like Julie Roginsky and Kirsten Powers stick to the facts and would never personalize an argument.

Then there are times like my years-ago appearance on *Hannity* with commentator Jehmu Greene. At one point during our debate on birth control and the war-on-women lie, she turned to me and let me know, "[y]ou wouldn't be where you are if it wasn't for birth control." The attack couldn't have been more personal and inaccurate. Who was she to insinuate that she knew any- thing about my background? She was out of line to intimate that it was birth control and not busting my butt for years in several different jobs that got me where I am today. I wasn't about to start discussing my sexual history on the air, especially with my mom in the studio that day!

I realized that I couldn't attack Jehmu on the air, at least not the way I wanted to in that moment. I could challenge her asser- tion, but I knew that I couldn't make mincemeat out of her. I'd just look like the stereotypical angry conservative. No one wants to see a bitch on TV. Republican women already had a reputation for being angry blondes. As a happy brunette, I'm not going to get branded any other way than as who I really am.

Untangling the anger knot took me a lot of time. I'm a passion- ate Greek and I'm intense. The subjects we discuss on Fox are not for the faint of heart: corruption running rampant in government; murderous radical Islamic jihadists killing and raping women; veterans dying because they can't get proper healthcare. It's diffi- cult to not lose your composure on air. If you really care about this country and the people in it, then you are going to have a reason to be pissed off. Some of the subjects make me so angry that it takes virtually superhuman strength to control my fury.

In fact it was Lou Dobbs who gave me some of the most useful advice in this regard. I passed him in the hallway one evening as I was heading to do *The O'Reilly Factor.* I had picked Lou's brain a few weeks before for career advice, so he felt comfortable stop- ping me to give me some more insight. "I thought of something," he said. He pulled me aside into the greenroom, where nobody could hear him. "Always remember to smile," he said (something, incidentally, that feminists go nuts over being told).

"Smile?"

"If you keep smiling that smile," he told me, "you can't lose."

I'm actually receptive to constructive criticism (again, unlike most feminists). I knew Lou was genuinely trying to help. He had been in the business a long time, and was very respected for a reason. I decided to follow his advice, and I try to follow it to this day. Whenever I get into a heated argument, even when I'm not on television, I always try to remind myself to make sure that the corners of my mouth go up a little bit. Even though I might be making very tough points, it doesn't have to look like I'm going to hurt someone.

As a woman you can ruin your reputation if you lose your composure even once, despite it being justifiable. I have a very low threshold for both incompetence and laziness, but I've conditioned myself to hold back my anger. When it gets really bad I have a little self-hypnosis mantra that I repeat: "Sunlight in, rainbows out. Sunlight in, rainbows out." Ladies: we should never act like Britt McHenry from ESPN.

Ironically what makes me most ticked off is that women have a different right to express anger than men do. I look at it this way. Feminists have long argued that often when men raise their voices it subtly contains a threat. Once again, the feminist answer isn't simply to stifle the male misbehavior—which they're trying to do by turning men into thumb-sucking wimps who watch *The Notebook*. Instead, feminists went ahead and adopted it as their own. There's no angrier, louder, more upset group of people than the crowd at a feminist rally.

The dynamic between women and our anger is an interesting one, because women are sometimes dismissed *unless* they're freaking out. It's like the other person doesn't consider a woman as actually angry until she's reaching a boiling point. Then and only then does her dissatisfaction warrant attention. Ironically, however, if you're screaming then the other person can't really hear you. They're more focused on the emotion or the tone than on what you have to say. This applies both in front of the cameras and in real life. We are constantly having to watch what we say and how and when we say it.

There is a silver lining here, however. As women get older, they begin to find the confidence to speak up for themselves in a way that gets their message across without getting fired or dumped. This is good because as we age there's more to get pissed off about—and few things infuriate women as much as the prying questions we get that men don't.

Women are *always* asked if they're dating anyone.

If we're in a relationship, then we're asked when we're getting married.

If we aren't married by a certain age, we get asked why.

If we get past a certain age then we're asked with that concern like we have some sort of disease, "Do you ever see yourself getting married?"

If we get married we're asked when we're having kids.

If we don't have kids right away we're asked if we want them.

If we have one we're asked when we're having the next one.

If we have two, we're asked if we're going to have more, which often forces us to disclose awkwardly, "Oh no, we're *done*."

While these questions seem innocent, they're often rude and inappropriate—and they are launched *constantly* by people who have no right to ask. We had a One Lucky Guy on *Outnumbered* ask me during a commercial break if I had frozen my eggs. Rather than reach across the couch and strangle him, I simply asked him if he had trouble obtaining and maintaining an erection. It's the perfect response.

Another One Lucky Guy asked a female host about having kids—right after she'd miscarried. He didn't know, and while he wasn't trying to be cruel I could tell that it cut like a knife. Men are oblivious to how common it is for pregnancies to go wrong, and they usually don't realize that women wait months before letting people know that they're expecting. These are intensely personal subjects that should be treated as such.

The problem is, the women aren't informing the men. We aren't drawing the boundaries. If that *Outnumbered* guest knew what he had done, he would have been mortified. As a result, these questions keep being put forth. I have a colleague who is known for asking prying personal questions. He always launches into a friendly but annoying interrogation every time I see him, which gives me angst.

When I was dating my boyfriend of five years he would always ask if we were getting married (we weren't and I knew it then). When I was dating the next one, he would ask when the guy was going to propose (toward the end of the relationship I knew he wasn't, and it was a source of frustration). When we broke up he grilled me on why and asked if I was dating someone. I always managed to deflect with cheery one-liners: "Life is good!" "I'm having fun!"

Each time I'd see my colleague, he'd make it a point to ask about the status of the relationship. He didn't ask because he cared; he asked because he used information as currency. If he cared, he would have asked how I felt after Dan died. Heck, if he cared he could have simply asked how *Outnumbered* was going. Instead, it was overly invasive.

I flashed my best Lou Dobbs–advised smile. "Don't take this the wrong way," I finally said, "but it's none of your business."

He was shocked at my response but knew that he had crossed a line. Most important, he never asked me again. It shouldn't

have to get to that point. But sometimes, rather than rip someone's head off and show anger, a woman can show firmness with
a knowing smile—and the F-word for effect.

While there is some acknowledgment in our culture of how
tricky it is for women to express either sadness or anger, what few
seem to have picked up on is that the other side of the coin isn't
any easier. Not only can't we cry, not only can't we yell—we can't
really express happiness, either.

I've always been a happy person, even as a child. Even though I
can be politically combative and personally competitive, I wasn't
someone who came in first place for everything. A lot of parents
tell their kids that it's okay to lose, but in my case my mom believed it—and so did I. Part of the reason I love my mother so
much is that I am painfully aware from talking to friends just
how badly poor mothering can mess someone up.

My mom raised me to be confident but not to be a total head
case. She never gave me the sort of neuroses that I think other
parents can. When I came back from living in Paris I was about
seven pounds heavier. On my five-four frame it made my body
look like an overstuffed French croissant. Rather than get upset,
I maintained that I still looked good and got to work to take
off the cheese-and-wine weight. I'm far from perfect, but I was
and still am *secure* with myself. As I got older, I saw that this
wasn't the norm at all—especially among women. Frankly, I feel
very fortunate to have been given this sort of mental framework.
Sometimes, however, it makes me feel like a bit of a freak. It's
almost as if being genuinely happy means that there's something
the matter with you.

Social media has certainly worsened this situation. Facebook
is a very dangerous tool to use, because so many people use it
to be manipulative instead of expressive. They're not showing
their life but trying to build an image. As a result, any time you

demonstrate joy on social media, it can be perceived as boastful. Insincerity is built into the site itself, starting from the fact that you can "like" something but can't "dislike" it.

I've had many friends counsel me not to post a lot of positive pictures on social media, because so many people are unhappy in their own lives. I don't know the exact proportion, but the vast majority of people really aren't cheerleaders for others, especially in my business. A chunk of them don't really care whether you're happy or not (which is of course their prerogative). Then there's the group who don't wish you well at all, as well as those who pretty much want you dead and will never be persuaded otherwise.

When I hear that women can have it all, I know it's not true. While women have accepted that they aren't going to be loved by everyone all the time, one of the things that's an indubitable reality is that women can't have the complete support of all their friends or coworkers when things are going well. It just doesn't work that way. People tend to like you more when you're down. This has nothing to do with you, and everything to do with *them*. It's their insecurity. You being more than makes them feel less than.

Whenever I find a loyal friend or colleague secure enough to lift me up both in bad times and in good, I never let them go. They're like pearls in a sea scattered with some empty oysters— but mostly filled with smelly clams. I love working on *Outnumbered* more than I've loved any job I've ever had—and I've had some great ones. I genuinely like and respect my cohosts. I'm happy with my man and have a great family, an airtight inner circle of loyal friends, a great apartment, and my health. I don't begrudge anyone else their happiness. Misery loves company. It's happiness that has trouble making friends.

I've learned that it's important to cover your candle. The less you tell people, the better. It's really kind of unbelievable, but

I've noticed a sort of complain, complain, complain conversational trend when women get together. While New York can be a miserable place for females to live, the women here aren't outliers. The *constant* griping that goes on here is part of an increasing modus operandi for our gender. The pressure is there, subtle and strong as female pressure tends to be. The more successful a woman, the more she is expected to bitch about the problems in her life to make her girlfriends comfortable. Otherwise they become targets for the group to take down. ("Who does she think she is?")

This is very much the case when it comes to women and our relationships. Married women feel the need to complain all the time. They're more interested in signaling their imperfections to their peers than in seeking support when things are in crisis. The husband does this one wrong thing or he doesn't do this one right thing. This sucks or that sucks. Frankly it all starts to run together in my ear after a while. So what if a guy left the toilet seat up? He didn't put a pipe bomb in the apartment. He's not having an affair—although *that* would be something women would actually keep to themselves. It's all for show.

Far too many women know what they want only by comparing themselves to others. "She's doing that. Therefore I need to do that." "She got a new dress. Therefore I need to get a new dress." This constant comparing triggers feelings of inadequacy, which in turn trigger feelings of depression. It's no coincidence that women are self-medicating in record numbers. "More Americans are on psychiatric medications than ever before," reports the *New York Times*. "At least one in four women in America now takes a psychiatric medication, compared with one in seven men."

Rather than seeking their own happiness, these types of women are living secondhand and taking their cues from others.

Worse, they tend to compare themselves precisely on those metrics where they themselves come off poorest. A wealthy, overweight woman will resent a poorer, thinner one for her build—while herself being envied for her money.

Yes, women are allowed to be happy about very limited, specific things. We can be happy about our careers *or* our kids *or* our marriages. But all three? No, that simply can't happen. That sounds downright inhuman. Yet there is one thing and only one thing that no woman can *ever* be happy with: her looks.

Chapter 7

Beautiful or Knot?

A MY SCHUMER IS always funny. She's hilarious when she's parroting liberal talking points on issues she knows nothing about, like gun control. But she's hysterical (pun intended, feminists!) when she's riffing on modern culture. A 2013 sketch from her show nailed it: "Look at your cute little dress!" one girl tells another.

"*Little?* I'm like a size one hundred now. Anyway, I paid like two dollars for it. It's probably made of old Burger King crowns."

When it comes to our appearances, women aren't just tied up in knots about their looks themselves—we're tied up in knots about discussing them to begin with. If any woman is content with her appearance, then she is to be hated and labeled a narcissist. In no other aspect of a woman's life is she so unable to be proud of herself. She can be proud of her husband and her children, or any other member of her family. She can be proud of her boss or her coworkers or her employees. She can be proud of keeping a lovely home, proud of her stylish wardrobe, proud of her career and her accomplishments. In each of these areas, a woman can not only be proud—she is *encouraged* to be proud, and to share her achievements with others. But not when it comes to beauty.

Looks are a knot all unto themselves. Not only can we never explicitly say that we're happy with our appearance, but we also can't allow anyone else to put that impression forward. Taking a compliment on her looks is one of the biggest things a woman can struggle with. Not because it's a huge struggle (this isn't exactly *Sophie's Choice*), but because it's such an impossibility to have an appropriate response.

No matter what the comment, the dance is the same. It's about downplaying, dismissing, and self-denigrating. Rather than accept the nice words, we have to delegitimize our appearance. If our hair is complimented for looking shiny we say it must be oily. If we're told our shade of nail polish looks nice, we respond by saying we could use a manicure because our nails are really a mess. Does a woman have a great smile? She'll let you know she gets it from her mom—that's who *really* has the great smile. Does a woman look thin or fit? Of course not. Looks like someone needs glasses. She hasn't been to the gym in a week!

A woman can't even say "thank you" when she gets a compliment. It would almost be like a tacit acknowledgment that (God forbid!) she agrees that her hair is great, that she has a beautiful smile or a fantastic ass. When a woman says "thank you," the complimenter hears "yeah, I know." And someone who knows that they look good is pretty much the dictionary definition of vain.

At the same time, there's a huge social push among some feminists for women to be happy with how they look. They've pushed to get pin-thin model types off the runway and more plus-size women on it. Famous women with curves like Beyoncé and Sofia Vergara are a far healthier body type to emulate than the super-skinny supermodels we were inundated with when I was growing up, like Kate Moss. This is a good thing. But we're at a point where female self-criticism is reaching insane levels. Women are no longer just comparing themselves to celebrities—they're comparing themselves to *Photoshopped* celebrities, a standard that the very same celebrities themselves are incapable of reaching.

Despite the useful message, this is only bringing about another dilemma. If everyone is beautiful but no one can say as much, there is still a lack of acceptable responses. Now every woman has to choose between biting her tongue about her beauty—or dissembling and saying that she doesn't think she is. We're either silencing women or turning them all into liars. It's a no-win scenario. This is one of the consequences of feminists trying to play a man's game on male terms. They don't know how to handle the issue of female beauty—traditionally and historically women's greatest strength.

This isn't something women can avoid grappling with. Women are constantly analyzing their own appearance. Even if we say that we're not, we are still cognizant of how we look. There's no woman who's completely fine with every single thing on her body and with her appearance. Every single person, man or woman, has something they're not happy with—but for a woman, that one thing far too often defines her self-image. Rather than being a beautiful woman with big thighs, she just sees herself as a big-thighed woman. The flaw eclipses the totality, and thus reality.

Sadly, women feel as if constantly expressing dissatisfaction with their appearance will endear other women to them. If a woman is weak and flawed, then other women won't hate her as much. In actuality that's not the case. Envy is never really about the woman herself. She's the object of the hatred but she's not the source of it—and in our society, no one is as objectified as attractive women are by other women. While men appreciate a hot woman, females want to decimate her. At least when men objectify women they still see us as desirable, as something positive. With women, the opposite is true. Girl power, my ass.

I know a woman who is blond, beautiful, and super fit. She
constantly has to hear little digs from the women around her. I've
witnessed it myself. It's never a direct insult, and I suspect that's
because these women are not always aware of what they're doing.
Rather it's veiled as "helpful" advice, like "those pants are too
tight." Once, one of her "friends" told her that she was too old to
be wearing a belly button piercing despite having a body so good
she could moonlight as a fitness model, six-pack abs included.
The advice was meant to undermine. "Don't listen to her," I said.
"She's just jealous she can't wear one. Don't let her make you feel
uncomfortable."

"I like my belly button ring," she explained. "I work hard for
this body and I think it looks sexy."

I could understand her mixed reaction. I've done the same
thing on dates. I constantly tried to not talk about success. I
felt a need to tame down any power that I had. Any comment
about looking good was my cue to tell that (true) story about the
time when I came back from Paris and had gained a bunch of
weight from constantly eating croissants. I thought I was making myself relatable to my dates. That's how delusional this sort
of thinking is. *Relatable?* What guy gains weight from eating
in Paris all day? And what guy would even care if he had? Guys
want confident, not cocky—but that's not something that most
women get till they get older. Now it's easier for me. If someone
tells me I look good I thank them. And usually add one word:
Pilates.

I'm not saying that there isn't room to acknowledge compliments in our culture—not yet, at least. But this song and dance
never makes things better and is a completely insincere waste of
time. A woman with a perfect smile—a smile I both lack and
am fine with—doesn't need to overexplain why her teeth look so
great. She doesn't need to prove to the other person that she isn't

vain, for the simple reason that she *can't*. That person is going to feel threatened regardless of whether the smile is natural or was shaped by braces. They're not going to feel comfortable with themselves no matter how screwed up they thought her grille might have been in the eighth grade.

I had to reassure my blond friend on more than one occasion to trust the mirror before she trusted those whispering in her ear (easier said than done). She had to become aware that it's almost impossible to find females who will sincerely build you up, especially when it comes to appearance. Women can genuinely be glad for your promotion, especially if they are in a different industry. But everybody's got thighs. Everybody's got an ass. Everybody's got hair. Bottom line: everyone's got issues.

Women's looks are constantly and ruthlessly analyzed—but when you work on television it's a whole other level of scrutiny. I don't mean just by viewers and commenters—the camera itself is completely unforgiving. If most women hate the mirror, imagine what it's like living in front of a distorting funhouse mirror. When I first started in TV, someone said I needed to lose ten to look like myself, because the camera adds ten pounds. Superthin women tend to look normal on TV. If you're short like me, you'd better learn to skip dessert. That may sound terrible, and feminists will be outraged that women in the public eye just can't be themselves because we have to focus on our looks. While it isn't fair, it's reality. *The Onion* joked that the unemployment rate of hot chicks is zero. It's funny because it's kinda true. We are an image-obsessed culture, and it's only getting worse no matter how much women's rights groups whine.

I'm not ashamed to say that I want to be my best self—*and I want people I care about to be their best selves, too.* When they ask me for advice (and *only* if they solicit it), I give them an honest opinion and actionable feedback. I tell them specific things they can do that will result in real positive change: a little Botox in the forehead; a reexamining of how they eat, because it's much harder to eat healthy than people realize; a workout regimen that they can actually stick to and fit into their busy schedule. As my mom would read to me from Proverbs, "Better are the wounds of a friend, than the deceitful kisses of an enemy." We are covered in kisses from enemies, especially when it comes to looks.

Women who work in television tend to downplay how much stress we're under. I get asked about it constantly, and it's a tough issue to grapple with. We're not just expected to look good; we're expected to be able to speak well and be prepared on any number of constantly changing topics. As much time as women on television spend reading up on the news, we also need to invest time in the gym *and* getting our hair done *and* getting spray tans *and* all the other things that come with the role. High-definition television is not the female's friend.

Television newswomen in *any* country don't look like ogres (for the most part). In fact, a good way to grasp a nation's standard of beauty is to look at who the newscasters are. It's an aesthetic business. They're not just there because they're good reporters. And to me, that's completely fair. It's not as if men are immune from this standard. Look at our own elected leaders. We haven't elected a bald president in sixty years. The last fat president was also the last president with facial hair: William Howard Taft, who left office more than a century ago. These things are inevitable in our culture. Women complain that it's really tough to age in television because guys have a longer shelf life. I get why they're upset. It's *not* fair—and neither is life.

We women also get far more feedback on our appearance than our male colleagues do—and the feedback is usually more negative than positive. If I've been up late at night writing and I'm a bit tired the next day, I'll almost certainly hear about it on Twitter. People will tell me to get to sleep earlier. If I gain weight I might get a tweet asking if I'm pregnant or telling me to lay off the cookies. The women have to try to look the same every day, to look consistently *good* every day, and that expectation is unmistakable when we've slipped from that standard.

Because the issue of appearance is so laden with taboo and emotion for women, it's very difficult to have open, honest conversations about it. I never had any true media training when I first started in television. I watched what other women on Fox News did and deduced that there were certain things that weren't going to work. There's a certain look that the audience has come to expect. I could tell that it was probably not a good idea to show up with, say, pink hair or over-the-knee boots. It takes quite a bit of time to take the TV template and put your own unique spin on it, just like anyone in any industry has to.

When I gain a pound or get a pimple, everyone sees it, thanks to the wonders of television. Obviously such concerns aren't unique to me. They're the polar opposite of unique, in fact. Every woman has knots about her appearance. To say that this shouldn't be the case might be true but it's also largely irrelevant. All the momentum has gone in the other direction, forcing us to care more and more. As proof, look up Michelle Obama on Wikipedia and see her great official photo—and then start going back through the previous first ladies. No one is putting Mrs. Andrew Johnson on television.

Few groups in our culture hammer women on our looks as much as feminists do. The same people who are supposed to be building us up are the very ones who most make us feel like crap about our appearance. The problem is the way we're wired. We're women. We can't help but care how we look—but this is an unforgivable sin in contemporary feminism. Feminists insist that we should want to be taken seriously, and apparently any attention to beauty negates that goal completely.

Fox News females get nailed for it all the time. No matter how many languages I speak or how many campaigns I've worked on, as a conservative woman at Fox I'm a bimbo to those who disagree with me. The looks of the women I work with are constantly being discussed and criticized. I once got an email from a girl in college. Her female professor was always making swipes at women who worked on Fox News, saying that we cared too much about our looks. The student decided to write a paper on why her professor was wrong. When she asked to interview me I told her to look at the women at networks outside Fox. It's not as if they were size sixteens with no makeup on and sweatpants.

There are gorgeous women at every on-air news outlet. It's a visual industry. Most women at Fox are lawyers, hold graduate degrees, or have other impressive resumes. The women I work with are smart and beautiful. What's so bad about that? Shouldn't women let women make their own decisions about appearance? If abortion is a woman's choice, shouldn't putting effort into our looks be considered an off-limits, harmless exercise? It makes no sense. A female professor teaching her female students to pick apart women on a news network for their looks flies in the face of everything feminism stands for.

Turns out, the professor agreed. She got an A.

If women are told not to apologize for success, then we shouldn't have to explain our desire to look good. Why do feminists get to cherry-pick the aspects of being a woman that are acceptable and those that aren't? In fact the very term *cherry-pick* literally speaks to the inescapable role of beauty in making decisions. The difference is this: smart women threaten men, but beautiful women threaten women. Once again we see that feminists are not actually interested in equality. They're comfortable with that which threatens men, and are primarily interested in things that serve the desires of women. Feminists will gladly shame women into not shaving. The theory is, who cares what men like? Be yourself. If he doesn't like it, it's his problem. Somehow *hygiene* is now considered submissive.

I once told a woman that I had spent three hours getting ready for a big date. She couldn't believe it and even lambasted me. "Why put in that kind of time? Either he likes you or he doesn't!" But women care what men think. We want them to think we're attractive—what women doesn't? So why are women shaming other women who try to look good if it makes them—and the guy they like—happy? If a man put in zero effort and looked overgrown and smelly, I'd never give him a second date. That's his choice. If a woman like Lena Dunham wants to look like George of the Jungle and not try, that's on her. Just leave the rest of us "Girls" alone.

Part of this escalating focus on appearance is due to the fact that we have more access to all sorts of images than ever before. In my mom's era, the only people she came into contact with were Lorraine the neighbor, Beverly down the street, "that awful Steph" at the PTA meeting—and whoever was on one of the three television channels at the time. Now anyone can see the appearance of just about everybody. There's no longer any need to wonder what Jay from high school looks like today. You can see his entire life on Facebook without even having to ask a common friend (and thereby showing your hand).

The problem is, everyone is well aware of this fact. So rather than focusing on being our best selves, many of us are interested in presenting a fictitious, heightened version of our lives. People can create a false impression that they're doing really well by, say, posting a picture of a car or a home that's not theirs. It used to be that only celebrities worried about their image. Now image— both literal and figurative—has become a near-universal concern.

This affects women differently than men, but it most seriously affects women from different generations. My friends and I never looked as good as the young girls I see nowadays. They look *beautiful*. They appear gorgeous and mature and hot because they have access to all the latest trends. We didn't have that. Pretty much the only cues I had to pick up on were *Seventeen* magazine, a trip to the mall to look at what other girls were doing, and my big sister Thea and her friends.

At seventeen years old, I never had Kendall Jenner's Instagram to look up to. There's a whole pack of young models like Gigi Hadid and singers like Taylor Swift who know what's up. Girls today are emulating young women who know what they're talking about. At our age, I think we were a little bit lost. We couldn't go to YouTube and get an infinite number of free tutorials on how to copy a celebrity's makeup.

There's another shift that occurred in the exact same timeframe. When I was a teen, supermodels were almost exclusively who you saw on the covers of fashion magazines. They were the ones who were pushed as the physical ideal. They took a lot of heat for that because most women could never make themselves into statuesque beauties who stood six feet tall. In a sense, there was less pressure because we could never really be Christy Turlington or Cindy Crawford or Naomi Campbell. The goal was unattainable, so why even try?

Now every fashion magazine puts celebrities on the cover— and not just the ones who won the genetic lottery in terms of bone structure. And it's not only magazines that give us our beauty cues. Regular girls who are into fitness or yoga can be elevated because of the Internet. I'm inspired by Instagram girls like Basebodybabes and Yoga_Girl. Friends of mine even keep Pinterest boards to get ideas for how to look.

There's definitely both good and bad aspects to these changes. With the increased information comes increased pressure. It's possible to ignore the psychological urge to look like Jessica Alba. She has unlimited amounts of money. She's got a staff—if not *teams*—of people to help her. She's got access to nutritionists and doctors. But the whole premise of inspirational Internet figures is that they're just the gal next door. Everyone has to do it.

One editor at a popular women's magazine told me that celebs make it look too easy and too perfect sometimes. There's no way they can raise two kids, be a size two, be an A-list actress, run a side company, have the perfect marriage, and cook every meal in their various houses while not one hair falls out of place. She knows they're bullshitting and simply won't print every line that gives the appearance of unrealistic perfection. (I thanked this woman profusely.)

It wasn't Kim Kardashian whose photo managed to "break the Internet." That honor surely must go to "Fit Mom" Maria Kang, who posted a photo of her ripped abs and three toddlers under a caption that read "What's your excuse?" Everyone lost their minds. "She's making us feel bad about ourselves!" women screamed from coast to coast. If some woman you never met is going to make you feel awful then don't look at her picture. Better yet, call a shrink. *Stop being a victim of other women's achievements.*

Social media is adding a whole other dimension to how knotted we are about how we look. Until quite recently it was easy to skirt looking perfect all the time. If you were feeling bloated, you could just miss that one barbecue or birthday party. If you didn't want to see anyone, you didn't have to. "Hey, whatever happened to Lisa? She just vanished!" Now that almost never happens. People are taking your picture whenever you go places—and then they post those pictures on Facebook or Instagram, often-times without your approval. If you look terrible in a picture, everyone is going to see it. Selfies have skewed how we look at each other and point to a larger obsession not just with docu-menting how we look at all times but with *self*. The ante has been upped almost everywhere to look perfect even when unfiltered.

In a quest for some semblance of authenticity, some teens are now creating fake Instagram accounts (or "Finstagrams"), ones where they can post pictures of themselves looking unfiltered, imperfect, and downright silly. They keep the accounts private and most are only followed by their closest friends. We would pass secret notes when I was in junior high school. Now visual messages are kept private so that friends can share moments without faking it in a quest to be perfect. It's teens fighting back to be authentic.

This pervasive obsession with looks has some serious social consequences. People are living longer and looking better doing it. Temptation abounds and social media is making it easier than ever to push out pictures that will get others' attention. People are getting divorced at high rates. These newly single women now have to compete with those who are a generation younger. Worse, this younger generation has far more knowledge when it comes to looking good—in addition to the natural beauty that comes with youth. How do you compete in a youth-obsessed culture? Be obsessed with looking younger. There are very few decent men who want a relationship, don't have a crazy porn addiction—yet are somehow available. If you're competing for them, you've really got to be on point. This is part of what's fu-eling the enormous increase in plastic surgery among men *and* women. They're willing to do and spend whatever it takes to have a chance in the dating pool.

Breast implants and Botox have all but become de rigueur.

Renowned Manhattan dermatologist Dr. Dendy Engelman informed me that the use of injectables has tripled in the last few years. For only a few hundred dollars, any woman can get her face all filled out. You don't have to go under the knife, you don't have to max out your bank account. The market is delivering to the consumer exactly what she wants, at ever-decreasing costs. It is the beauty of capitalism in the flesh. Pun intended.

Like anything that makes you feel good, the aesthetic alterations can be addicting. Women are going as far as to get Botox in their elbows to get rid of wrinkles. There's a new procedure in Manhattan called Blowtox: the woman gets Botox injected into her scalp so she doesn't sweat when she works out; that way she preserves her blowout. The *New York Times* reported that searches for butt implants have increased exponentially. Surgeries like labiaplasty (where a women has her outer labia trimmed to have a more perfect package) are on the rise, as is vaginal rejuvenation (a procedure that firms up the vaginal canal). As my newly single friend told me, "After my divorce, I needed a tighter business plan."

What we're now seeing is that plastic surgery has trends precisely like hair and fashion do. Dr. Allen Rosen of the American Society of Plastic Surgeons told me that "keeping up with the Joneses" (and, no doubt, the Kardashians) is a huge reason why women are getting work done. "Mommy makeovers" are huge. If one mom in the Hamptons or at the Jersey Shore gets a tummy tuck, then all her friends—and frenemies—are sure to notice. Instead of asking where she got her dress, they'll find out where she got rid of her belly.

If a person is willing to literally reshape her body, then very frequently she will start reexamining every aspect of her life. Plastic surgery used to be about fixing insecurity. (Actually it was originally about repairing war injuries, but that's ancient history at this point!) Now, it's often about being self-obsessed. If she can do better in the mirror, maybe she can do better in the rest of her life—including her marriage. Dr. Rosen has seen many husbands talk their wives out of getting work done because they're scared that the Mrs. will look better and reevaluate her options. These men aren't paranoiacs. This sort of thing actually happens every single day, as women trade in their wedding band for a boob job. Dr. Rosen sees it all the time.

For the first time, women who connect with Middle America are openly talking about cosmetic surgery. As a prime example, Courteney Cox and Kelly Ripa talked about how much they love Botox. That's the stamp of approval for any woman to go do it. As plastic surgery grows more accessible and acceptable, we are seeing an unprecedented approach to the end goal for women and their looks.

Until very recently, plastic surgery was meant to look as realistic as possible. In the New York City plastic surgery scene (yes, it differs by city, just as fashion does) that's still largely the agenda. Women want to have, for example, natural-looking breasts. They don't want to look overdone. They want every change to be slight. But in California and—to a lesser extent—Miami, they want to look done and *over*done. They want big, high breasts. They want huge, puffy trout pouts.

No matter what city, these women have something in common: they want to look *young*. They want young-looking skin, young-looking faces, young-looking butts—and young-looking *everything*. It's almost a complete taboo to mention what happens to a woman's private parts after pregnancy and childbirth. It's also almost a complete taboo to discuss the fact that women are increasingly going under the knife to do something about it. We are still in a time where labia can't be mentioned in many media contexts—but we will soon be at the point where they will be the talk of the town. Yippee.

The argument used to be that this was all a mild form of mental illness. These types of women were existentially unhappy, they couldn't handle getting older, they needed therapy and not surgery. It's not that simple. To be nonpartisan, both Michelle Obama and Laura Bush wear tasteful, flawless makeup. As historian Thaddeus Russell points out, a century ago any female with even their amount of makeup would have been looked upon as a literal prostitute. Beauty standards do change, and have been doing so for decades. To say plastic surgery is crazy is simply untrue. The data shows that, if anything, plastic surgery–driven women have a *more* objective grasp of reality than their critics do.

I recently saw a survey in a women's magazine that took men of every age and showed them women's pictures. The magazine wanted to pin down what was perceived to be the ideal age for a woman. To little surprise, twenty-one-year-old guys liked twenty-one-year-old girls. But what was surprising is that thirty-year-old guys liked women of a range . . . from twenty-one to twenty-three. The researchers went all the way up to sixty-year-old men. The outcome was always the same: They want the girl who is between twenty-one and twenty-three. Depressing stuff, I know.

So what can women who are my age do about this fact? Sure, we can unsubscribe from the magazine immediately so that another weekend isn't ruined. Yes, we can contemplate shooting ourselves in the mouth before realizing that's just a permanent solution to a permanent, ever-worsening problem. I don't know that there *is* an answer. I do know that berating men that this is somehow "wrong" (that is, something feminists don't want to be

true but nevertheless is) simply won't work. At some point, haranguing a heterosexual man and telling him not to be attracted
to a tight, young woman becomes like haranguing a homosexual
man and telling him not to be attracted to a tight, young guy.
Ideology can't trump sexual desire, regardless of whether it is informed by biblical fundamentalism or base feminism. You can't
persuade an organ that can't even hear you.

The good news is that technology is giving women the ability
to look better as we get older. Pair that with the confidence that
women have as they age and it's a potent combination that my
straight British hairdresser Kieran says is irresistible. "There is
nothing hotter than a confident woman. One who knows what
she wants, is comfortable in her own skin, knows her body, and
knows how to use it. The younger girls may have hot bodies but
they don't know how to use them." I know I feel far more confident and comfortable in my skin than I did a decade ago, but
I still apply sunscreen and anti-aging serum to that skin every
single day to prevent signs of premature aging.

I'll freely admit that the idea of getting older isn't a pleasant
one. I think lots of women fret about looking in the mirror and
seeing someone they don't recognize. In one of her songs, Lana
Del Rey asks, "Will you still love me when I'm not young and
beautiful?" Unlike Del Rey, most women are too scared to admit that they're scared. After all, fear is a girly symbol of weakness. But I don't think it's an irrational fear. Getting freaked out
by a gray hair isn't the same thing as getting freaked out by a
mouse. The first time I saw a mouse I was startled. The first time
I *thought* I saw a gray hair I almost had a nervous breakdown.
Thankfully it was only blond, but the crisis wasn't averted—it
was only postponed. That first gray hair is undeniable objective
biological proof that a woman is aging.

I'm in my midthirties and small things have already started to fall away. I can't do splits like I used to when I was a gymnast. I can't do certain things in workout classes. I've resigned myself to the fact that I'll never be able to do a back handspring again. Is never being able to do a back tuck again going to negatively affect my life in any way? Of course not. (Maybe my husband's. Wink-wink.) But all those things are going to start adding up. It's only downhill from here. Older people all say the same thing: getting old sucks.

For me, one of the worst parts of getting old isn't waiting for lines to come in on my face or hunting for gray hair. If I could somehow become twenty years younger, I don't know that I would. Sure, I would be able to do literal backflips and could wear different outfits. But while being younger might be great, being younger nowadays isn't. When I think about being younger, I don't reminisce about my youthful figure. Sure, my body was younger, but my life is way better *now*. The drinks have gotten better, the clothes have gotten better, the housing has gotten better, and the vacations have gotten better. But not everything is better. When I do get nostalgic I think of how people used to interact and how men approached women and dating. The young women of today sure might look better than me and my generation ever did—but they're not *living* better at all.

Chapter 8

Knots of Intimacy

TOO MUCH OF anything can be a bad thing. Even otherwise good activities can quickly become downright dangerous in excess: too much work, too much play, too much sleep, too much exercise. But only one of these things is so dangerous that it has its own moniker: TMI. In the book of Genesis, the serpent tempted Eve by leading her to the tree of knowledge (aka, information) despite being warned against it. She didn't listen—and we all know how things ended when Adam later followed. I suppose you could say that "too much information" was the original sin.

Nowadays, there's another serpent leading innocent young women down a tragic path: Lena Dunham. It's easy for conservatives to dismiss Dunham as a child of privilege, but that's grossly unfair. Her connections might have gotten her in the door, but she's the one who took it and ran with it. She deserves credit for being undeniably talented. Her big breakthrough as a contemporary feminist icon was as the writer and lead actor of *Girls*, a popular show on HBO. The series touches on many issues. Some of it rings true, and some of it is just insane.

Let me explain a couple of issues where Lena Dunham deserves applause. We've heard people speak of "the fog of war."

Well, there's also the fog of rape. It *isn't* always black-and-white, and it *can* be shades of gray. In fact, that's what they call it: gray rape. Dunham is absolutely, 100 percent right: it's real, and it's a real problem. Men are so conditioned to getting sex that even if a girl tries to resist, she will likely be pressured into it. There have been many times I've heard a friend say, "I can't go out with him tonight. He'll expect sex, and I won't be able to say no."

Dunham also hits the nail on the head when she says there is ageism against women in their twenties. I am not sure that will ever go away. If you are young and female (and especially if you look good) you will be perceived as less competent and/or intelligent than a man with the same training and qualifications. It isn't until our early to midthirties where we start to get treated like we're seasoned and know a thing or two.

If only her show were as insightful as these two points. Her *Girls* character Hannah protested the very idea of TMI. "By the way, TMI is such an outdated concept. There's no such thing as too much information. This is the information age!" In *Not That Kind of Girl*, Dunham wrote that "when men share their experiences it's bravery, but when women do it it's some sort of—people are like 'TMI.' I feel like there is some sense that society trivializes female experiences." There is, and Dunham is a root cause.

No one has had their trivial experiences elevated to the level of national importance by the media like Lena Dunham. Dunham is a thread in a larger quilt of cultural dysfunction. We are part of a society that thrives on trivial information: *Huffington Post*: Burrito blamed for bus crash. *Los Angeles Times*: One-legged dog and a chicken become best friends. New York *Daily News*: Man with nineteen-inch penis says it's too big to work. But for a woman who claims that she wants women to be taken seriously, Dunham does females few favors.

Taking herself quite literally about there being no such thing as TMI, Dunham decided to devote an entire chapter of her book to what she eats. She feels that what she eats is so . . . important? . . . interesting? . . . special? . . . that everyone needs to know about it. Why should I care what Lena Dunham eats? I care what Jillian Michaels eats. I care what Heidi Klum eats. Maybe there *is* a reason why I should care what Lena Dunham eats. Maybe certain foods inspire her to write better. But I don't know why I should care, because Dunham herself never cares to explain—in other words, there's too little *actual* information, and plenty of mere data. TMUI: Too much useless information.

From the press that she got—until she turned radioactive, that is—Dunham was practically regarded as a contemporary goddess of wisdom. She thought she could say whatever she wanted and receive enormous adulation. But despite the media attempts to paint her as the transcendent voice of a generation, it's painfully obvious that this Athena of absurdity didn't exactly spring forth fully formed from the head of Zeus. Something had to make her this way—and that something was her parents.

Dunham's father was an artist who drew pictures of women's vaginas. The mom was also very liberal. In her book Dunham admits that her mother never corrected her and never told her anything was wrong. Neither parent ever disciplined her or set boundaries. Dunham was, as she put it, "allowed to do whatever she wanted." Nothing was considered inappropriate in that household (except perhaps reading The Federalist unironically).

This is the backdrop that allowed a young Dunham to think it a fine idea to see rocks in her sister's vagina—and to think nothing of writing about it as an adult with no sense of pain or fear or guilt. (That's not to mention the anecdotes about Dunham masturbating in the same bed as her sister.) There's no way that most siblings raised by parents who set boundaries would have been able to conduct the same behavior and not suffer the consequences in the form of some sort of discipline.

Any psychologist would call this disturbing behavior. Not only are such behaviors clearly not right on their face, but they also point to deeper underlying issues and dynamics. After a certain age, they would even be criminal. Yet Dunham didn't really need a shrink or a defense attorney. What she needed was a sense of right and wrong inculcated from her parents. Now the woman with no sense of right and wrong has become a moral compass for an entire generation of millennials. Apparently the Outback Steakhouse isn't the only place whose motto is No Rules, Just Right.

Of course someone who was raised free-to-be, as Dunham was, would insist that there's no such thing as TMI. At no point in her life would such a perspective ever be challenged. She did all these awful things when she was a kid, and then no one disciplined her for them. So what happened when she got older? Ta-da! We got someone with a complete sense of moral relativism, one that depends solely on what *she* thinks is right. She lived in judgment from no one. Not even the media called her out, because no one read her book.

There are only two people who really bothered to look with any sort of critical eye at what the *Girls* creator actually wrote: Breitbart editor at large Ben Shapiro and myself. It was Shapiro who finally said, "Wait a minute. Some of this behavior is really disturbing." I went after her on television in the same vein. Not only should she not have done those things, but she didn't need to share them with the world. So what was Dunham's reaction to the growing criticism? Rather than be the strong woman she claims to be, her reaction was trite and predictable: "I'm a victim. Stop attacking me."

Here again we see that feminists are not really all that interested in gender equality. In fact, the only time most feminists *are* silent is when there is a gender disadvantage that favors women over men. If Lena Dunham had been male she'd never have gotten away with any of those acts. Molesting your sister and committing lewd sexual behavior in a bed next to her would be understood as child abuse, and every feminist would be up in arms over this Duggar Family 2.0. "Leon" Dunham would be sitting down for a television interview and people would be calling for his show to be canceled. *Girls* would have been pulled from the air if it had been called *Boys*.

Yet the problem isn't just Lena Dunham's actions. It's how her perspective informs her show, which had been touted as a sort of modern manual for younger girls. In fact, *Girls* was presented as a successor to *Sex and the City*, but there are some very profound, disturbing differences. Our culture has coarsened so quickly that even a show with the word *sex* in the title now comes off as relatively conservative.

Sex and the City definitely pushed the idea that there is "too much information." The series examined things like saying too much to a guy, or saying too much to *anyone* (or showing too much skin in different scenarios). The show taught the girls of my generation that it's called "overkill" for a reason. These issues were debated by the cast. Inevitably, however, it demonstrated different repercussions for the characters' behavior. The message was that there *should* be some sort of boundary, because if you do certain things then other things will happen. In other words, it repeated the conservative mantra that actions have consequences. At the same time, the viewer was left to decide what would be the right decision for the character to make—the conservative mantra of personal responsibility.

Girls is different. *Girls* is the Lena Dunham show from start to finish, and frankly, Lena Dunham herself is the Lena Dunham show pretty much all the time now. She constantly puts it all out

there. Whether it's nudity or nonsense, everything is okay because Lena Dunham says so. It's her rules and that's how it's going to be. In her world there have never been any consequences:
not now, not ever. In the real world, there are consequences, and
big ones. It's a dangerous message to convey to people, and especially to "the weaker sex."

Children need boundaries, and adults—men and women
alike—need boundaries. Saying that there's no such thing as
TMI is not only the wrong message—it's demonstrably false.
Boundaries are criteria for appropriate behavior. "I was assaulted"
and "I like corn" are not equally important statements in any
context. If everything is of import—at least of enough import to
tell people—then nothing really is.

Thanks to social media, everybody now has a fair shot to share
whatever they want. While it gives everyone a voice, it elevates
the irrelevant to a level of importance reserved for the relevant.
Then we need to sort through it. Not everything everyone shares
is worthwhile. Some of it is also inappropriate. It is impossible for
anyone—even Lena Dunham—to read through a Twitter stream
without pausing fairly frequently to wonder, *Why did you share
that?* I'm guilty of it myself. I'll tweet a picture of me eating guacamole. Why would anyone care if I'm eating guacamole? In fact
there is nothing more uninteresting than me eating guacamole.
But then again, *I'm just eating guacamole.* I'm not half-naked,
smoking a joint with a remnant of cocaine in the background, in
a picture I just posted—like Miley Cyrus has done.

Feminists like Lena Dunham are the *first* to dismiss the voices
of people they don't like. Their definition of TMI is information
that is critical of them in any way—which to them means any
comment that falls short of the fawning support they believe
they're entitled to. Criticizing a feminist at this point is hate
speech and practically akin to assault.

My boundaries were set firmly and fairly when I was a kid. I learned that not everything I had to say was that important, and that not everything I had to say was okay. If I got too disrespectful or hurtful with my comments, then I would be eating the back of my dad's hand or my mom would be looking for the wooden spoon to spank me with. If I *still* didn't learn my lesson then my mom would take away my phone privileges and forbid any visits with my friends. If I couldn't talk then I couldn't have fun. Getting a playdate or sleepover canceled felt like death—but it taught me the importance of biting my tongue. It was a very crucial lesson for me—a professional bigmouth—to learn.

Feminists like to say that those who argue for boundaries with regards to, say, sex are actually antisex, antiwoman, or . . . too conservative. That's just a rhetorical trick to avoid discussion by attacking the messenger. To carry the metaphor further, I think it's pretty clear that I like information. I like talking, and I like communication. Yet I'm arguing that there most certainly is such a thing as TMI, and feminists are tied up in knots because they're uncomfortable *ever* telling women to not speak—unless it's me, whom they have no problem telling to shut up.

The term *TMI* doesn't just apply to Facebook status updates or Twitter posts. They say that a picture is worth a thousand words, and there's absolutely no doubt that photographs are enormously informative. It's one thing to know that Bruce Jenner is transitioning; it's another thing to see Caitlyn in a dress and a faceful of makeup. That's why the paparazzi make so much money. Photographs and visuals in general say things that prose simply can't.

But is it really an unmitigated good to share something that your significant other or your kids wouldn't want you to? I've seen moms posting pictures of themselves on Facebook in "MILF" T-shirts. I'm arguing that that crosses a line, because that's embarrassing to the kids. That self-identified MILF isn't the one who has to deal with the whispers in the hallway—or the teachers who might see the photo. She just thinks she's hot, and if anyone else has a problem that's on them, right? Hardly.

I have to give feminists credit: at least they're consistent in also advocating for *visual* TMI. Dunham herself is constantly naked on her show, for no apparent reason. She can't even explain why, other than that she just feels like doing it. This is what happens when there are no boundaries to determine behavior. We're reduced to the level of a three-year-old who likes running around the house without any clothes on just because. It's not empowering; it's infantilizing. There's a reason the show is called *Girls* and not *Women*.

TMI necessarily leads to TLI—too little intimacy. I don't mean romantic intimacy here. I mean the intimacy of two friends sharing personal information and helping one another. *Everyone* needs that sort of relationship in their life. The television series *Entourage* was based on the very well-established idea that powerful people need allies around them lest they go crazy. Even President Obama had Reggie Love on staff for just that purpose. If there are no boundaries, if I'm telling everybody everything, then the things that I tell my very close friends mean nothing. If I tell my friends nothing, then my relationships are without intimacy. *If there's no intimacy, then there's no real relationship.*

If feminists like Lena Dunham admitted that there's such a thing as too much information, they'd have to establish some criteria for judging the quality of the information they're putting out. Then they'd be in real trouble, because so much of the information that they're spouting is unmitigated crap.

This oversharing on social media is destroying relationships. It feels like everyone else has it better than you, or that everyone else has it figured out, which in turn is leading to collective moments of unhappiness. You can't change how posting photos will make someone feel. When I read studies about how Facebook is making people jealous of their friends, I have a very simple response: find some new friends. But most social media accounts are rarely about a person's real friends. Instead, users want to rack up as many "friends" as possible. My dad used to tell me that if I was lucky enough to die with one or two really good friends, then I would be lucky. But imagine a Facebook account with only two friends? You'd look like Agent Loser. Most social media "friends" are anything but. Of course they aren't going to wish you well.

Social media antagonizes this destructive aspect of human nature. Oversharing and posting every single moment of your life has led to women questioning why their friends "liked Sarah's picture on Instagram but not my picture." If someone doesn't follow you on Instagram then they aren't your friend, according to modern standards. Not tagging someone in a post is akin to not wanting to be associated with them, even if you just forgot. All across the country, high school girls are getting in fights because a friend will post a picture at the mall with another girl when she said she would be home studying. "Why is she at the mall with Stacey? Just yesterday she told me she hated Stacey. Now they're shopping together!" "There is this feeling that everyone has it better," Jane Buckingham, founder and president of consumer insights firm Trendera, told me. "The ability to be friends is a lot harder."

I found this out firsthand.

One summer I was at the beach with a good friend of mine, Julia. We posted a few pictures of us together having fun. "Cristina unfollowed me on Instagram," she told me.

"Why?" I asked.

"I think she's jealous I'm here with you."

Weeks later, an acquaintance of both of us didn't just unfollow Julia and me. She blocked us, perhaps the most aggressive of moves in today's social media melee. I supposed she couldn't accept the fact she wasn't included in the fun—but that would have been the case with or without Instagram.

The same thing goes for men and women. If you text a friend or a love interest and they don't respond to a text you sent but they have time to tweet or post a photo, it feels like you're being ignored or aren't important. "Why isn't he texting me back? I know he's on his phone. He just tweeted something about the New York Giants game!"

We know everything about one another by one click, including who other people's friends are. You used to have to find out these things organically or by having an actual conversation. Now the door is wide open for misinterpretation and constant miscommunication in an era where nobody communicates anymore. Miscommunication was hilarious on every episode of *Three's Company*, but in real life it ain't so damn funny. We're oversharing under the guise that we're all communicating, but nobody is really communicating *authentically* at all. TMI makes the ability to be a friend or a lover a lot harder. We're all getting meaner, and we're getting harder on each other. As if love and friendship weren't hard enough. Then, add the ability to quit, defriend, unfollow, block, or delete anyone or anything from your life and you have a world in which it's really easy for people to not honor their word. We don't have to commit to anything: plans, pictures, purchases. Everything is so *temporary*.

For feminists, women should be able to do whatever they want, whenever they want. This naturally leads to things like the recent "free the nipple" movement. Apparently a woman should be allowed to walk down the streets of Manhattan completely topless if she wants to. Of course, it's not simply the *legal* right to do so that feminists are asking for. That would be far too sane. No, they want women to be able to walk down the street and have no men notice. No staring, and *definitely* no hooting and hollering. If a guy takes a picture? Why, that's practically a hate crime.

The question I have is simple: *Why?* Why do feminists want women to be allowed to walk down the street topless? The feminist answer is also simple: because guys can. Men also pee standing up. I don't want to do that. I don't want to use a urinal just because men get to do it. Wanting to do something simply because others are doing it is the lamest of excuses that teenagers give their parents. So why have women based an entire movement around it? The fact that we're in a *nipple competition* shows how far we've veered off course as a culture and how low contemporary feminist discourse has fallen.

Rather than developing their own standards, feminists simply look to see what men do and try to mimic it. In my view, women shouldn't be looking to men as guides for how to behave. If anything, it's *men* who should be looking to *women* as guides for what *not* to do. The argument is that women should be able to do what the guys do because we should have the same privileges as them. This is where feminism really took a major misstep.

A lot of the things that the men were doing weren't right. *It wasn't ever okay.* There simply wasn't anyone to aptly criticize them because men sort of ruled the world. Now women have become the rulers, the oppressors. It used to be the man who was seen ordering the woman around. Now it's the woman in the driver's seat. I once saw a sign that read: "The opinions expressed by the husband in this house are not necessarily those of management." Wasn't that the main gripe of feminists, that men were the managers and rulemakers of us? Now it's only our way or the highway and *he* doesn't get a say? So much for equal rights.

When feminists like Dunham aren't putting men down they're far more interested in being edgy provocateurs than in making the world a better place. To them *homemaker* is a four-letter word. Instead of focusing on making the world a better place for both genders, they choose to focus on making the world an equally terrible, morally corrupt place, all in the name of fairness—and both genders are paying the price.

Nowadays there's pressure for girls to put everything out there and to constantly up the ante. The men certainly aren't complaining, and the women don't want to complain, either. Everyone has a smartphone and everyone's on social media. Everyone is posting pictures of themselves—and looking to everyone else for where the boundaries are. Yet it seems that no one has any clue, and the only people speaking on the subject are saying that boundaries shouldn't exist.

There's an idea in fashion that you can show boobs *or* you can show legs. If you show both, it tends to look pretty slutty. You have to pick one to accentuate. Even if I weren't on TV, I would be careful about what I post. As a former political press secretary, I carefully managed the images of my bosses and of candidates. I know that lines are drawn for a reason, and I treat my life the same way. I'm always asking myself if a pic I'm posting is appropriate. Is it too risqué? Is there too much skin? If there's any doubt, I don't post it. The same goes with my words on Twitter. I think it's important for viewers to see and hear my thoughts off-air, ones that don't always have to do with politics. I post pictures to prove that I'm not always in a jewel-toned polyblend dress. Even though I keep my posts classy, there are people who think I show too much. There are *always* going to be people who are offended by something you do.

Yet younger women are asking themselves less and less often what is appropriate. The mass oversharing is less of a filter and more of a free pass: If she's doing it then I can. They don't even know that there's such a thing as too much skin, and I doubt any of their parents are telling them that there is. The ones who are digging in their heels against such trends are only being ostracized for it. They're not getting the attention from guys, they're not getting the validation from their classmates, and they're not really keeping up with their peers.

I can vividly recall going to the Preakness Stakes in 2002, right after graduating college. Though the backdrop is a horse race, the Preakness is actually a huge party. In the center ring especially it's complete mayhem and malarkey, with drugs and alcohol. Near me there was a girl from a different sorority than mine. The guys were chanting all around her: "Show your T-I-T-S! Show your T-I-T-S!" It was exactly like a *Girls Gone Wild* video or those cringe-worthy clips from spring break that Jesse Watters airs on *Watters World*.

The girl was beautiful and very voluptuous, with a great body. She also happened to be drunk, so she did what the guys wanted. The response was positive and overwhelming. As I stood there, hearing all the guys cheer, I realized that this was something that I would never do. Even if I wanted to, even if I thought it could be fun, and even if I thought my boobs looked every bit as good as hers, I would always have a little voice in my brain telling me not to do it. What if I got a job someday, and it came back to haunt me?

I'm sure that this girl didn't actually experience many repercussions. If there was a picture of her, it would have been taken with an old-school camera or a disposable one. If someone wanted to duplicate it, they'd have to find it and then scan it in. Now, however, it's a much different story. If a girl did that nowadays, she'd be done. The pictures would be all over her college or even high school.

The cost of uploading the picture is the press of one button.

The cost of duplicating the picture is the press of one button.

The cost of sending the picture is the press of one button.

The cost of saving the picture in perpetuity is the press of one button.

It literally takes more effort to call someone—dialing seven numbers—than it does to send everyone in your social network topless photos of a drunk girl flashing her breasts. And once those pictures are up there, they're there in perpetuity. It's a common sitcom device for the uptight mom to have secretly been a hellion as a young girl. Soon that joke won't be able to work anymore. The Internet never forgets. Our pasts will be captured in perpetuity, and publicly so.

I'm not saying this to chastise these young girls. Everyone is dumb in high school. Everyone makes stupid mistakes. The problem is that they don't understand they're going to be paying for these mistakes for years to come. They're going to apply to colleges. They're going to apply for jobs. If I were a boss and saw a picture of a sixteen-year-old girl half-naked at Coachella, I might have a little bit of a question about her hireability. It's not a question about her being loose, either. Every job entails some measure of discretion. People tend not to hire employees who don't care about the rules—or who can't seem to understand why they should.

The timeframe for consequences to manifest is also compressing. Young women don't have to wait until a prospective employer googles them to face repercussions. That's so five years ago. My intern related the story of a girl she knew who sexted a naked picture to a guy. This sixteen-year-old dude—being an immature jerk, as sixteen-year-old dudes are wont to be—pressed one button and forwarded the picture on to some people.

He didn't even need to have malicious intent. Maybe he wanted to look like a stud in front of his friends. To him it simply wasn't a big deal. After all, there's naked pictures all over the Internet. What's one more? And if wasn't a big deal to him, it sure wasn't a big deal for *them* to forward it on.

The girl fell into the throes of depression, complete with an eating disorder. Then she became downright suicidal as the photo went viral. All it takes is one person to know someone at another high school for a whole new audience to find the pic—and that's exactly what happened. How are she, her parents, or the school supposed to get this picture off the Internet? It's impossible.

The Lena Dunhams of the world would blame the girl. She should get over herself. She's only uptight, right? "Lighten up, toots! There's no such thing as TMI. You should be proud of your body!" Rather than encouraging modesty, these types of feminists are encouraging *more* nudity. My question: what's left? If our breasts should be totally fair game for pictures, if there should be topless parks, are we just keeping our bikini bottoms on for now? Even Vice media put out an article last fall that asked, "Why are films so afraid of showing vaginas?" We can't stop this hedonistic decay when feminists are taking the proverbial slippery slope, and going down it in lingerie.

If I post a picture of myself from the back on the beach on Instagram, the comments are incessant: "Turn around." "Let's see the front." It's not enough skin, and it's never going to be enough skin. What feminists seem to be completely unable to understand is this: *Having shame is not the same thing as being ashamed.*

A female nipple isn't just a man's nipple. Sure, they look the same—but they're not looked at the same. Men are still turned on by the female breast. They look at us differently than we look at them. There's nothing wrong with modesty. There's nothing wrong with mystery. It's why people watch and read mysteries:

because they *are* exciting. Take the mystery out and there goes the excitement with it. This idea that women should be able to do whatever they want with no consequences, that they should be able to send a naked picture with no consequences, is absurd. Keeping something private actually takes incredible control, and control is real power.

Here's why it's going to get worse. It's one thing to tell young women that they don't have boundaries and can do whatever they feel like doing. It's another thing to *encourage* them to do things that were previously unthinkable. Permission becomes persuasion and then ends as expectation. Boundaries are like walls. They are necessary. There's a certain freedom in knowing what one will and won't tolerate, and the path that a person is going to take. But for today's young women, there is one industry whose current standards are becoming tomorrow's demands: pornography.

Chapter 9

Fifty States of Gray

THIRTY MILLION PEOPLE worldwide are watching porn at this very second, at *any* given second. But when I was growing up, there were many social and technical barriers between a would-be viewer and the product. If you wanted to watch porn you had to go to one of those weird, windowless buildings out by the airport. They even had makeshift wooden fences in the middle of the parking lot to keep who was entering and exiting a secret.

I'm not nostalgic for the shoddy neon signs flashing "peep show," "XXX," and "private rooms" in the window of places with names like the Playtime Boutique. Every once in a while I'd catch a glimpse of some guy—*never* a woman—on his way in or coming out. I'd always think, *Ew, what a creep!* Then there were the back rooms of the video stores, with wooden beads separating the regular movie section from the "adults only" nook. Occasionally I'd catch a glimpse of a man or a couple emerging from therein, trying to hide the disguised copy of whatever funnily titled movie they were renting. If you wanted to be dirty, you had to deal with the stigma. It took effort to get dirty on the down-low.

The mainstreaming of porn was gradual and consistent, but there were definitely spikes when the changes happened quicker than others. In 1990, MTV banned Madonna's video for her song "Justify My Love." Undeterred, she released it as the first-ever video single, going on to sell half a million copies. Looking at it now on YouTube, it's mind-boggling to think that ultraliberal MTV ever had a problem with it. It's also mind-boggling to understand how so many people felt the need and desire to spend money to own the videotape. Neither of those behaviors makes sense in today's technological and social context.

The Material Girl followed up her video with the 1992 book *Sex*. It was considered so outrageous that it came wrapped in a Mylar cover, and was sold under the counter at the bookstore. *Sex* went on to become the best-selling coffee table book of all time, and topped the *New York Times* bestseller list. Now the content is considered a big yawn compared to what one can find online, for free, in a fraction of a second.

I remember an episode of *Friends* from the ancient times (1998) in which Chandler and Joey's television accidentally started delivering them porn for free. They were too scared to change the channel or turn off the TV, lest the porn—this scarce, precious commodity—vanish and be lost forever. There were some definite moments of cultural pushback, which imply that this wasn't all inevitable. Despite Larry Flynt's best efforts, in the 1990s Rudy Giuliani made a name for himself by shutting down the smut boutiques of Manhattan—changing the entire dynamic of the city. But since then the momentum has overwhelmingly been in the other direction.

Today there is a twenty-four-hour, seemingly endless buffet of every kind of free porn fetish: girl-on-girl, amputee, pregnancy. What used to be underground is now mainstream. The Internet even has a term for this effect. So-called Rule 34 states, "If it exists, there's porn of it." As technology has become more accessible, we've become more libertine, more hedonistic, and more sex obsessed. The distribution model has gone from smut parlors to buying or ordering videotapes to direct digital downloads. There's no longer any risk of someone you know catching you purchasing a dirty magazine. Gone are the days when the porn companies had to spell out to the consumer that their products are mailed in discreet envelopes. Now everything can be done in the privacy of the consumer's home. *Playboy* isn't doing nudes anymore; the pornographic pioneer can no longer compete. In the blink of an eye we went from soft, pretty nudes to full-blown spread eagle.

It doesn't just have to be on the laptop, either. We're in a world where everybody can get porn on their cell phone. Most guys I know are downloading porn on their phones the same way that people digest the news. You can follow specific porn stars on Twitter and Instagram, so you don't even have to search for it. Erotic videos are now dumped in your feed with the same frequency as breaking news stories, making every smartphone into a potential smutphone.

As technology has changed, so too has the nature of the porn that people are consuming. Before iTunes, you had to buy an entire album to hear a song (except for those few released as singles). Porn is going the same way. Porn consumers don't want to spend the money on an entire feature because they don't really care about the plot lines, lines that weren't exactly that thick to begin with: "Oh, our tennis partners didn't show up. What do we do now?" (Spoiler: they have sex.) Now the performers are just getting right to it by selling individual scenes.

Pornographic subject matter is rapidly changing as well. The *New York Times* had an article about how Americans search online for sex, and what the most common Web results are. (FYI: "Big booty" is on the rise.) It's not just butts and boobs anymore; those are ubiquitous. It's gotten into young girls, which had been very taboo. There's also a trend for selling videos of first-time auditions. In the same way that *Big Brother* gave us a window into a household, these videos give us a window into the casting process. You can actually watch a girl permanently lose an aspect of her innocence without getting up from your sofa, at a cost that is prohibitive to no one.

What if an aspiring porn starlet doesn't make the cut? All it takes to become a XXX girl is a webcam and a laptop. She can film Web clips either by herself or with one or more partners, post the clips online, and get paid based on downloads. The more clips she posts, the more skin she shows, the more graphic it is, the more money she's making. Or she can have people log in to pay to watch her do things on a video stream. These "cam girls" become more popular the more that they're willing to push the envelope. The more they're willing to specialize in things that others aren't, the greater their reward.

Anyone can be a pornographer, and any girl can be a porn star. In fact, some girls are enlisting their boyfriends to act as the male in the clips. This new strain of at-home porn that's dominating the industry doesn't need Los Angeles or Silicon Valley. These women can be anywhere. It's given Big Porn quite a bit of competition.

As the nature of pornography has changed, so too has the definition of it. I remember walking down the streets of New York more than a decade ago and noticing how the dirty magazines at the newsstands would be obscured. At street kiosks, the pornography would be in the back, usually wrapped in plastic.

When a pregnant Demi Moore bared all on *Vanity Fair* it was a national story. Today you can find most women half-naked on magazine covers. Nipples project through see-through tops, whereas they used to be airbrushed out. Bare bottoms are front and center whereas they used to be blurred out or reserved for *Playboy*. Every mall in America has shopping bags from

Abercrombie, replete with male nudity and pubic hair. We're so completely desensitized that we've all forgotten that what used to be viewed as porn is now just . . . a picture.

Under the fairly recent definition of the term, pornography has become ubiquitous. It's there in the simulation of sex on award shows. It's the Kardashians taking *constant* nude risqué selfies. It's Lindsay Lohan and Miley Cyrus taking topless pics that in the past would have been banned. There used to be the blurred, checkered, digitized bar over the chest area. Now the body-painting series *Skin Wars*, for example, shows full female top-lessness every week during prime-time television. I'm not saying toplessness is terrible. I'm not saying *Skin Wars* is evil, since the show does it in a largely tasteful way. I'm simply saying that the cultural norms have clearly changed. The series is doing some-thing that would have recently been unthinkable, and there is absolutely no reaction. No one has apparently noticed this shift.

I don't believe that any and all change is inherently good. Nor do I believe that all positive change is positive through and through. Sometimes positive change brings with it lesser nega-tive consequences. But we have to first register that a change has occurred before we can assess its impact.

Despite all the above, I'm not interested in judging people's porn consumption. That's not my point or my desire. I don't em-brace the typical conservative view that porn is entirely pure evil and that we're all slouching toward Gomorrah because of it. It's not a black-and-white issue. Porn can ruin intimacy between two people. It can also enhance it. Frankly it depends on the couple, and it depends on what and how much they are watching. I'll leave that to the sexperts. I believe the best way to maintain intimacy is to keep pornography out of a relationship altogether. The mind and the imagination are powerful tools.

Yet, just as with other repetitive, unhealthy types of consumption, porn and the single man can clearly become a problem. That's not to say that women don't look at porn, because we do. But the frequency and voracious appetite that leads to addiction is mostly male. While the sex therapists whom I've talked to acknowledge that masturbation is healthy, they also concur that it can become highly antisocial behavior by its very nature.

If someone is constantly pleasuring themselves alone instead of engaging in sexual activity—instead of *connecting* with another person—there is a clear lack of intimacy. It creates a vacuum where chemistry and human connection used to be. It's called "intercourse" because there is meant to be an *exchange*. It's meant to be a duet, not a constant solo performance.

Porn can become so addictive that a guy can't have sex without it. In one episode of *Sex and the City* Miranda started dating a man who had to put on his favorite porn films while they were having sex. Instead of looking at her, he would stare past at the images on the TV behind her. When she told him to make a choice between her or the videos, he responded, "I just met you. Some of the women in these videos I've known for years."

Men have grown to count on certain things from women in the bedroom. If they see something on television—or on their laptop, or on their smartphone—that looks fun and different, they're going to want to try it. It's given rise to the mainstreaming of things that used to be considered illicit. Men increasingly view choking as part of intercourse, and the unprecedented success of *Fifty Shades of Grey* is encouraging them to act more like Christian Grey—if not Chris Brown.

Violence is entering the bedroom at a time when violence against women is getting more attention than ever. On one hand, women are (rightly) up in arms about sexual assault, but on the other they made the Fifty Shades trilogy a billion-dollar enterprise and were buying up rope in hardware stores across the country to be restrained and mistreated willingly during sex. It's no wonder men and women are confused.

More men and women are seeking out group sex options instead of one-on-one play. There are sections on Craigslist designed just for these types of encounters. On October 13, 2015, the *New York Post* reported that the inventors of a new app designed to make threesomes happen raised $500,000. Even "open relationships" have become more mainstream, with outlets like Vice giving advice on how to have a nonmonogamous partnership: "You can be polyamorous, a swinger, a friend with benefits, in an open relationship." According to Vice—though not the dictionary—these all fall under "the new monogamy." As I type this, my word processing program doesn't recognize the very word "polyamorous." How long do we have before that is something everyone is familiar with? Two years, if that?

It is a novel idea to try to rebrand these types of relationships as monogamy. It's also a way to normalize people's perversions and give them an excuse not to make or honor their commitments, or to have any self-control. I couldn't care less what people do in their bedrooms. It's none of my damn business. But I do know this: monogamy can be hard. There is a lot of temptation at our fingertips. I also know that, as a cultural observer, for every action there is a cultural reaction.

Like everything else, we want an easy way out and so the culture is creating a shortcut. But with that shortcut comes a sharp lessening of the bond that is formed with two people, whether for a few months or forever. If everyone is having sex with everyone and there are no boundaries, no monogamy, no intimacy, we are losing pretty powerful stuff. We're headed toward a host of other problems. So we're all going to be screwing each other and life is going to be great?

Removing intimacy from the equation brings forth a culture

so coarse that it seems almost impossible to change direction. Then we have to factor in other natural emotions, like jealousy, insecurity, and paranoia. One fairly liberal psychologist I spoke to said that after thirty years of treating patients she has never once seen an open relationship thrive. The whole nonmonogamy thing is, in her view, "a bunch of bullshit."

Whatever the inspiration for the new monogamy (that is, the old polyamory), whether it's porn or just boredom with things that are routine, the rise of accessible and raunchy porn has inspired us to be less socially stable. Whether the act is group sex or some other lewd act, the women in pornographic videos are paid professionals. There is no emotion exchanged—just fluids and money. When the scene ends there is no envy, no feeling of betrayal. It doesn't work that way in real life. If men and women are emulating what they see online, they'll find it's impossible to replicate it without consequence.

Most women are not professional porn stars, whether physically or just emotionally. I've talked to more than one woman who feels that guys today expect the same bedroom gymnastic performances they see in clips and on websites, and they are tying themselves up in knots—literally and figuratively—to satisfy the guys. For the first time, it is *women* who are having performance anxiety in the bedroom. This worry about being less than was unheard-of for females. It was something that for millennia had been the exclusive domain of men. We're not just keeping up with the Joneses. We're keeping up with Debbie, too—and she's done an entire city in Texas (whereas we can barely do the laundry and find time for a manicure).

The porn standard has permeated to female grooming as well. The 2011 movie *Bridesmaids* has a scene where Maya Rudolph's character has an argument with Kristen Wiig's, who had been her best friend. Wiig is jealous of Rudolph's new bestie (Rose

Byrne) and is upset that the two of them apparently went to get their buttholes bleached together. Rudolph, nonplussed, admits to doing the deed—and furthermore, says that she happens to like it. Worrying about one's butt hair was once strictly reserved for porn stars. Now strategic and puzzling product placement of this trend has convinced women that they have a problem they literally can't even see for themselves.

There is an entire faction of the feminist movement that loathes the porn industry and believes that it objectifies and denigrates women. There is a lot of truth to that. But my concern is more about how it's affecting regular women and their relationships. I once had a guy I interviewed tell me that he looks at porn every morning while he drinks his coffee and reads the paper. "I have it on in the background. I'm not doing anything sexual at the breakfast table. I just like to see what new videos are out there." He eventually admitted the videos were of first-time auditions, which led to an interest in watching much younger girls having sex with far older men. Then he started having sex with much younger girls, something he hadn't been doing before. Clearly, this is a chicken-and-egg thing. But just as clearly, those "eggs" wouldn't have been on the menu twenty years ago.

Women have told me story after story of how guys today have tried to emulate things that they've seen online. The details are too graphic to write. Many probably think that while the women are suffering, the men are winning. This is temporarily true, but it's not a long-term scenario. Younger men today are consuming so much pornography that they're having trouble having normal sex with a normal woman. This is causing extreme emotional damage and intimacy issues.

Let's examine how something as benign as taking a bikini photo has changed within the last couple of decades. Before, you would take the picture . . . and then you would have to wait to get the film developed. You would go to the Kodak center or the supermarket to get it developed and printed out. Then you'd have to wait to pick it up. If you were lucky there would be a one-hour photo place where you "only" had to wait sixty minutes. Truly we were living in an age of miracles when *that* innovation occurred. Finally, you got the pics. If you liked any, you'd get a couple of copies of them.

Let me take this one step further. Imagine if a girl ran to Kinko's immediately afterward in order to make hundreds of copies of her bikini photo to give to every person she knew. That would have been insane. The thought process of any such picture recipient would be the same: "Wow, she loves herself." "She's really self-obsessed." "She thinks she has a great butt." "*Why is she handing me this photo???*"

That behavior is no longer considered crazy. It's considered your Instagram game. In fact, many people have bikini shots as their profile pic on various sites (and not just dating sites, mind you). It's the first thing a stranger sees of them. Everyone feels pressured to do it. If you do have a good figure, you still feel like you have to keep up with what all your peers are doing. If you don't, you'll feel like there's something the matter with you. I'm as guilty of these feelings as any woman. I have a few bathing suit pics on my Instagram, but my body parts remain in my bikini. While I may be frolicking in the sand, I also draw a line in it. Other girls may not have that line, and so they're putting everything out there.

How did this happen? If someone had come along and tried to consciously turn American women into a nation of porn stars, they wouldn't have been able to do it. No leader is that charismatic or persuasive on their own. There were several recent steps. In 2007—those bygone days when Barack Obama was first running for president—Kim Kardashian one-upped her good friend Paris Hilton. Whereas Paris was "famous for being famous," it was the leak of the Kim/Ray J sex tape that made the Kardashian name so well known. She literally became famous for being an amateur porn star, whereas having a porn past used to be the kiss of death for aspiring celebrities.

Kim is very much a symbol of American culture, both good and bad. She didn't want that tape to go public—but once it did, she decided that she might as well make money off it. That same year she was ambivalent about posing for *Playboy*—but her mother, Kris Jenner, pushed her to. At one point she did still have something of a filter. All women do, much more than men. Women ask themselves the same constant questions: "Is this right?" "Should I do this?" "Is this too much?" In response to these concerns, our culture is ripping down boundaries and saying, "Just do it." If the Statue of Liberty were a real woman, she'd be half-naked by now.

On a personal level, once the dam has been breached, there's very little that one can do to fix it. In 2014, Kim decided to bare all for *Paper* magazine. Her choice is perfectly understandable: why develop modesty now? In my view, that was a pivotal moment in the coarsening of our culture. The rollout was strategic and transparently so. One day she's on the cover showing her bare butt. Three days later came the breasts. Finally came the full-frontal pictures she had posed for, and which she knew would eventually be released.

For one week straight, Americans weren't talking about the rise of ISIS anymore. We weren't talking about the danger of Iran becoming nuclear, or about how veterans were dying because they couldn't get proper medical care. No, for that week the entire country was discussing Kim Kardashian's ass. That's what was trending. That was the big focal point. That's where we were as a nation.

That full frontal pic was showing up in my Twitter feed whether I wanted it to or not, and it wasn't blurred. It's at the point where people who don't want to see porn can't help but see it. The old argument—which is not entirely untrue—was, "Don't like it? Change the channel!" But you can't change the channel on a Twitter or Instagram feed. They are, by their very nature, a compilation of many people's individual "channels." Sure, you can unsubscribe or block individual users. But there's nothing you can do during a week where everyone is retweeting the same explicit images. Pornography has not only become mainstream, it's become inevitable—and unavoidable.

The crucial key to the Kim Kardashian saga is that none of this behavior hurt her career. In fact, the moral (pun intended) of her story is that she essentially became famous for a sex tape. It was the launching point for her and her entire family. They've done a lot with their fame since then, but the only person in that entire household who had done anything of worth was former Olympic athlete Bruce Jenner. Which is the greater accomplishment: winning the decathlon, or making a sex tape?

That's again part of the problem. It's very easy to make a sex tape these days. It's even easier to duplicate it. It's a very troubling situation when there's no moral compass anymore. No one even focused on the betrayal of intimacy that Ray J committed against Kim. Violation? Huh? What "violation"? She should have known better than to make the tape. As I point out constantly, bad decisions inevitably lead to bad consequences. That doesn't mean that the person—in this case, Ray J—who visited said consequences upon the woman is some kind of saint. There's plenty of blame to go around.

This combination of no boundaries and the encouragement of every girl to act like a porn star has disempowered women—and handed men a very dangerous weapon. If a girl asked me for my advice, I would tell her that she should never send someone an explicit photo. She should definitely not make a sex tape, no matter what reassurances she gets from the guy. Even if he's trustworthy, that video can still be stolen. Computers can be hacked. For the girls, there's often shame involved from a leaked tape. For the guys, there aren't a lot of penalties. This asymmetry has led to the existence of a nasty form of social behavior called revenge porn.

Imagine a guy and a girl in a relationship. They're happy and in love, and neither ever imagines breaking up with the other. The guy asks the girl for an explicit photo, something involving nudity or some sexual act. Since all her friends are doing it without repercussions, it doesn't seem that big of a deal. There's an old expression that hell hath no fury like a woman scorned. But a scorned man with a smartphone doesn't have to have his proverbial panties in a bunch to go on the warpath. All that has to happen is he needs to think, for literally one second, that forwarding this picture to other people is not only acceptable but a good idea. No one can argue that such an act isn't hurtful and humiliating and a betrayal—but no one can really figure out how to stop what happens next. Even if the guy is legally punished, the photo is out there and can't be unsent.

No women are more revered and more powerful than Hollywood celebrities. In 2014 several of them, including Kate Upton and Jennifer Lawrence, had their phones hacked. Completely naked photos of themselves were released on the Internet for all the world to see. These women were in a bit of a conundrum. They couldn't say with a straight face that there was anything wrong with the photos themselves. Any girl knows that a picture is only on your phone if you think it looks good. No woman is going to keep a crappy naked selfie on her cell. She would delete it immediately.

So instead the actresses kept talking about betrayal and their loss of privacy—when that very privacy is something that many young American women are *choosing* to throw out the window every single day. They don't seem to think that it's a problem. Even if they did, there's nothing they could do to reverse things. Jennifer Lawrence had access to the best legal team that money could buy. Every guy I knew had found every single naked photo of every celebrity before they got "taken down" (that is, made marginally harder to find). If Lawrence and her powerful peers couldn't do anything about it, then the average young woman has absolutely no chance.

Celebrity in many ways anticipates typical American life. Jennifer Aniston gets a new hairstyle, and then every woman in the 1990s is sporting "the Rachel." It works this way with music, with clothes, with jewelry—and with all aspects of appearance. This is why the Jennifer Lawrence hack was so chilling. She didn't want those pictures out there and she deserved her privacy. But for every Lawrence, there's a Cyrus.

Miley Cyrus takes naked pictures of herself and puts them on Twitter and Facebook. She can claim that she's not a role model, but that's absurd given how our culture operates. I'm not even castigating what she does per se. If she wants to self-destruct, that's her dilemma. No one is forcing her to (literally) broadcast the fact that she uses hard drugs. This is clearly a choice that Cyrus is making. All that does is motivate younger girls, and validate that it's okay to follow in her footsteps. The mainstreaming of nudity, narcotics, and a lack of privacy is certain to lead to the breakdown of norms. Rallying behind all of these things at once can't help but produce profound cultural effects.

It doesn't have to be this way. This approach is *not* inevitable. Taylor Swift, for example, is exponentially more successful than Miley Cyrus. But Swift doesn't feel the need to take pictures of her naked behind, or put her sexual activity online. She leads with her voice. She demonstrates that you can be demure and modest—and still be a success even in our culture. Kim Kardashian was known only for being naked on film. Swift is legitimately known for being amazing on every recording she does, with her clothes on. I'm sure Swift has, say, gotten drunk on many occasions. But I have to guess at that, because she chooses not to broadcast that information. If there was a sex tape of hers, she'd be mortified as opposed to selling it.

Some argue that all this is largely a function of technology, that attacking pornographic levels of nudity is like 1890s beachgoers being mortified by the sight of a woman's ankles. To me, that sounds a bit like Aesop's fable about the sour grapes. In that fable, a fox is desperate to reach a bunch of grapes that are high up on a vine. Unable to do so, he walks away, convincing himself that they must have been sour anyway. In other words, if you can't have something, it's probably bad to begin with.

This argument of inevitability is the opposite of the fable. It says that if we have no choice but to be nude, if we have no choice but to expose every aspect of our selves, if we have no choice but to take our cues from the pornographic and pedophilic, then whatever ensues *must* be good. We assure ourselves that the change is what we wanted all along, simply because we don't see an alternative. The grapes must be sweet simply because they're so in reach. If everyone's doing it, it must be great, right? *Right?*

It's one thing to pressure young women to expose themselves

emotionally and physically. The problem is, what happens when their conscience kicks in? Everyone has a line that they draw within themselves, a line past which they aren't comfortable. Are we respecting those lines, or are our cultural figures fighting desperately to obliterate them? In my view, it's clearly the latter. Our young women are told to put it all out there without considering the consequences.

And then they're told not to care.

Chapter 10

Above the Fray

MY FRIEND CORA is a pretty cool girl. I set her up with a friend of a friend named Jake. They both were around the same age and I thought they had a lot in common. Jake reached out to Cora after I had passed along her picture and her phone number. They spent hours texting. Soon hours turned into days, and days into almost two weeks.

"What's the deal with Jake?" I eventually asked.

"He texts me all the time," Cora explained, "but he hasn't made a plan to ask me out."

The Dr. Tantaros diagnosis: Failure to Launch Syndrome ("FLS"). I followed up with Jake's friend to get him to make a move. "Tell Jake that when guys take too long to ask women out, it takes the air out of our balloon, *capisce?* Texting gets annoying. She's going to lose interest."

"Ugh," he groaned. "I got it. I'll tell him."

Soon after, Jake made a plan with Cora for drinks. They clicked—and then went right back to texting. A week later, he finally mustered up the manhood to ask her to meet. Was it dinner? A movie, perhaps? No, it was an invitation to meet him and some friends who were already out partying. How . . . romantic.

At first Cora passed. While she's classy enough to know this isn't the way to court a nice girl, and smart enough to know that meeting a guy and all his buddies isn't the best second date, she was cool enough not to specifically state those two aforementioned points. Jake didn't ask her to dinner or for drinks again. Another week of texting ensued. Lo and behold, the next ask was the same: meet him and his friends out.

Even though Cora was annoyed, she decided to join them. She did like Jake, and against her better judgment overlooked her trepidation. As the evening went on he proceeded to get completely inebriated in front of her. By the end of the night Jake was falling-down drunk. His friends had left and the bartender was motioning her to get him out of there. That wasn't a big deal. After all, Cora drinks. Who cares if he got drunk in front of her? Not Cora, because she's a pretty cool girl.

Worried he could end up dead in the street, Cora decided to chaperone the blackout-drunk guy home. He was, of course, too inebriated to fool around, which technically meant it wasn't a one-night stand. Even if it had been, who cares? Even if she had *wanted* to have one and couldn't, who cares about that, either? Not cool, man. Not cool.

Prince Charming woke up in the middle of the night not once but twice. The first time, he couldn't find the bathroom. That wasn't a big deal. After all, Cora didn't know where the bathroom was in his apartment, either. The second time, he thought he was in the bathroom but he was actually in the corner of his bedroom. Who cares? Cora's been lost *tons* of times.

Throughout the course of the night, Mr. Manners peed on his radiator *twice*. Now, Cora might have been a pretty cool girl but she had never done that—but again, she's a girl and girls can't really pee on radiators. It would be far too difficult for her to get a good mount on top of all those pipes or slots or whatever they're called (Cora wasn't a heating engineer and neither am I).

Her loverboy even managed to pee his pants in the bed when she was lying next to him. She didn't want to be judgey—we've all peed the bed at some point. Sure, most of us were under the age of five, but being young is cool, right? He was like, being retro and ironic.

The next morning, Cora didn't want things to be awkward with the guy who might still be her boyfriend one day (or not, who cares?), which might lead to marriage (if he's into that sort of thing) and then children (no one's thinking that far off, relax!). She hadn't gotten up and left the first time he'd peed the radiator. She hadn't gotten up and left the second time. What, was she going to make a scene in the morning? Not a chance. That would be uncool. She'd made her bed, he'd made it wet, and now she was going to lie in it. Everything was fine. The only one who was pissed was the sheets.

To make it clear to the distinguished gentleman that she didn't think he had a drinking problem (at least he *drank* out of the correct receptacle) and that she didn't think he was a boorish cad, Cora made it a point to make a joke. "You sleep okay?" That way, Aquaman would know that she's cool—and every guy just wants a cool girl to settle down with. Just ask them.

Cora was wasting her breath. The guy, archenemy of dry radiators everywhere, didn't even care that it had happened. He wasn't embarrassed. Why would he be? If *she* didn't care, *he* sure as hell couldn't be expected to. Cora continued to text with Jake after that and managed to get hung up on him over the ensuing months, never once calling him out on his consistently bad behavior. One night it was not making a plan to go out on a date; the next he would text—before ghosting her for a couple of days, then reemerging. Then she heard rumors he was on a dating app. Hmm, that didn't seem all that cool.

How could Cora *possibly* have foreseen that Jake would be a jerk? She never even told herself, half the time. She, like millions of women today, was just too cool to care about that sort of thing. The result was that she was always rewarding his bad behavior by pretending that she didn't care when in fact she knew he was a drunken cad. She not only convinced him she didn't care, she convinced *herself*.

Dating has become so challenging and the culture so perverse, that when women find a semidecent guy who checks some boxes, they tend to overlook some of the most critical nonnegotiables. Women are forgiving things that they would never consider justifying before, just so they can have someone. It isn't just my friend Cora. This problem is rampant and it's not just in big cities like New York. Women aren't speaking up when guys deserve to be checked. Guys who have cheated are excused by women because "the relationship wasn't clearly defined." Guys who have acted beyond immature are excused because they "will grow up eventually." Guys who have set off red flags everywhere have women from coast to coast shouting "look at all the pretty red flags" instead of running the other way.

I am as guilty of this as anyone. I should have left the man I came close to marrying way before I did. He never cheated or lied—that I knew of—but he wasn't marriage material, either, not for me and not for anyone. Instead of challenging the way he acted, I overlooked it. I told myself it would be different once we settled down, while knowing and fearing deep down that it wouldn't be. Instead, I wasted my time and my energy. I'm so conditioned to keep my cool at work that letting it slip off camera is hard to do.

Some women make excuses for their relationships or decide to play it cool because they fear being alone. Those were not my failings in this situation. I don't mind being alone. For me, the driven modern woman, I desperately wanted to make things work so that the relationship could be a success. Pulling the plug would somehow be a failure, as opposed to cutting my losses. I was confident that I could change him . . . because I was cool enough to do it. Or so I convinced myself.

One consequence of the power trade that feminists made was that women decided to become more like men. That included adopting male techniques, including their laissez-faire approach to love. Most men don't care about the same things that women care about. They generally aren't emotional creatures. In trying to act more like men and less like women, many women—especially young women—have tried to adopt an indifferent, dismissive male mentality.

There's a great deal of buzz in Internet culture about the alpha man and what he stands for. He sure doesn't get hung up on emotion. He *definitely* doesn't get hung up on one woman. If a girl is seen with another guy, he shrugs. If a girl cheats on him, he might break up with her—but he won't lose any sleep over it. The alpha man rises above it all. He's above the fray.

This mimicking of the illusive alpha man is one part of the puzzle. But there's another paradigm at work here: Seth Rogen's archetypal character in the movie *Knocked Up*. To be clear, there isn't enough beer in America to make me sleep with Seth Rogen. There aren't enough narcotics or narcotics combined with alcohol to make that happen. The film has a plotline where the gorgeous Katherine Heigl gets drunk and sleeps with him, only to find herself pregnant. It's more fantasy than comedy.

Throughout this Judd Apatow production—the man who works with Lena Dunham on *Girls*—Rogen spends his time sitting around taking bong hits with his friends as they watch DVDs to see when the characters get naked. Heigl gets increasingly frustrated with him. When she tells him that she's pregnant, he doesn't really take it very seriously. He keeps on smoking pot and looking for boobs on the television. There's no manning up whatsoever.

Heigl ends up internalizing her feelings. She doesn't freak out when she learns that she's pregnant, at least not for quite a while. Nor does she freak out when she learns that she's pregnant with Seth Rogen's baby, which is perhaps the most horrific movie pregnancy since Mia Farrow played Rosemary. In real life, a marginally sane woman who becomes pregnant from a guy who just sits around taking bong hits is going to care about it. She will not last through a few months and then have a freak-out on their way to the doctor's office. Yet Heigl's character—the one who is portrayed as having it together in the relationship—doesn't lose her mind. A cool girl is too cool to even care about things like getting knocked up, and with whom. The movie's tone is one of humor but the subtext is one of horror: *In Apatow's America girls don't care about anything.*

This affectation isn't limited to intimate relationships with men (let alone any actual romantic ones, in the rare cases that those still occur). With girls in their twenties, it's also permeated their interactions with their female friends. Everything can be and is frequently dismissed with one simple word: *whatever.* The more I hear about this occurring with younger women, the sadder it makes me feel. An editor at a big women's magazine confirmed this phenomenon to me over drinks. "Girls aren't saying what they really want or mean," she said. "They want to act just like the guys: drink beer, chill. Be above it all. If anyone does anything to upset them, they never show it. They are too cool to care."

Every person deserves one friend they can be themselves with. Every woman needs someone in her life that she can *care* to, whether it's about a guy not calling her back, or a guy deciding that he wants to date somebody else, or declining to commit. She needs someone she can be her authentic self with. She needs to be able to say, "You know what? I can't believe he's not calling me back. Why isn't he calling me back? What an a-hole! I really liked him."

Nowadays it's one girl asking another girl if she ever heard from some dude. Every "no" is immediately followed by a declaration of indifference—in other words, by a lie. Ninety-nine percent of women care, but we *pretend* like we don't. Competition is so fierce among women that we've convinced ourselves that emotion equals weakness, that saying what we really want is a flaw. As a consequence we aren't only losing authenticity between the genders: women are losing it with other women. I dread going to dinner with some of the women on the periphery of my life, because I already know that the conversation will be superficial and pointless. I'm not going to tell them what's authentically going on in my life and they're not going to tell me. The same dialogue is repeated every day by women throughout America:

"How's everything?"

"Great."

"Your friends great?"

"Great."

"Great."

"Everything's great with me, too."

"That's great."

"Check, please."

What a waste of time. Life's too short for two things: wasted time and crappy drinks.

It isn't just with women that I'm not showing my true feelings. I'm guilty of invoking the too-cool-to-care strategy in my romantic relationships as well. It's led to dozens of miscommunications with men and lots of wasted time. Rather than tell them how I really feel or what I'm really thinking, I shelve my emotions for fear of losing them or being vulnerable, which could lead to rejection.

I've had three long-term boyfriends since I was twenty-three years old. While I had no trouble telling the first one how I felt, as I got older I found it much harder. When I look back I recall thinking that if I upset my first I actually didn't care. If he was offended by me bringing issues to light then he could take a hike. People in their early twenties think they're invincible, and I was no different. There were single men lining up to date me. If my boyfriend wasn't on point with his behavior and how he treated me—or if I confessed my love for him and he rejected me—I didn't care. Sure it would hurt, but I would move on and *fast*. The loss was his and his alone.

Typically a woman is supposed to gain more confidence and get more vocal as she matures, and she does in many ways. She'll do it at brunch or a baby shower but not when it comes to matters of the heart. So why are so many of us regressing? It's mind-boggling. Smart, strong, accomplished women are not being completely candid with guys because they do not want to be vulnerable or alone. Vulnerability means taking a risk. Will the other person be sympathetic? Will they see your side of things? If you like a guy and make an effort to tell him how you feel, there's a chance he won't feel the same. And to many women—myself included—there is nothing worse than the feeling of rejection.

As a woman who has come into her own, this fear of being vulnerable feeds into a subject that many of us constantly avoid nowadays: monogamy. It's something that most women want but are pretending to be too cool to ask for. During date number two with a man I really liked, I wanted to ask him to not see other people. But every time I imagined saying it, I couldn't do it. Even though I liked him, I kept questioning myself, *Is it too soon to ask? Will he be freaked out? Will he think I'm moving too fast and get scared?* I just didn't want him to say no. Another part of me felt that it would make me look soft. God forbid Andrea Tantaros look soft, or reveal to a man that she cares about him before he does. That would mean that I lose, and he . . . wins? Now I realize that when you find the right one, there is no worry about winning or losing. In fact, the games go away altogether.

I didn't say it made sense, people. This is my knot, one I tied in my mind. In hindsight, worrying about all those things involved me asking all the *wrong* questions. Who cares what he wants? Who cares if he is freaked out? If he is, then *hasta la vista.* If he isn't, then we *both* get what we want. But by staying silent, we both might *not* be getting what we want—or he's getting what he wants, while I, the female, am not.

I let this relationship drag on, assuming we were monogamous but never having the conversation. It led to worry on my part, and one massive miscommunication. A picture I saw online showed him with another girl, who I assumed was someone else he was dating. Rather than ask who she was—can't do that because that would show I *care*!—I decided to go on a date with someone else. When he found out about my date he assumed that it was *I* who wasn't monogamous. He decided to ask me about it weeks later, after I shared with him that I missed him. "Aren't you seeing that other guy?" he demanded.

I was stunned. "Well, aren't *you* seeing other people?"

"No, I'm not."

I felt stupid. The girl in his pic had been a friend, but my date wasn't.

"Andrea, if you wanted this with me, why didn't you tell me sooner? I'm hearing this for the first time and we've been dating for awhile. This changes everything." So much for assuming he didn't want monogamy. Guess that old saying is true: when you assume, you make an ass out of "u" and "me." Only in this case, it was mostly me. And girls, make sure you understand this: guys will rarely make a case for monogamy unless you mandate it. It's just not how they're wired. So you give them the choice, and if they don't take it, you know early on that you are worthy of more and can move on.

Dozens of girls have told me similar stories. They catch the guy they're seeing on a dating site and fail to call him on it. Then the behavior gets overlooked, and it gets repeated. They want marriage and children but don't want to ask too quickly if the guy wants the same things. That makes women sound desperate, and desperate is not cool. Girls want to be free, fun, and loose. Young women want to be that girl who is so down with whatever, so chill, that the guy will *want* to hang around her because she's so cool. Trust me on this one, girls: *it never works.* I'm not advocating losing your mind on him, but I am advocating being true to yourself. (And I've only now started to untie this knot myself.) If you're not, you will waste time, precious time that as a female you don't have—especially if you want to have children eventually.

I frequently speak to groups of female interns or college students. I always ask them what goals they have so that I can offer useful, applicable advice. When I ask who wants a career, the response from the group is inevitably close to unanimous. They all want careers, and they're all driven and ambitious. Then I mix it up and ask them a question they hadn't expected: "Who wants to get married or have kids?"

Silence.

Their eyes dart around the room, with no one wanting to be the first to raise her hand. They don't know what to do, regardless of their stance on the matter. It's like playing the drinking game "Never Have I Ever," where one person throws out a scenario ("Never have I ever walked in on my parents") and whoever has experienced the situation needs to take a drink. Even if you had, it's terrifying to admit it—and for today's young women, it's terrifying to admit that you want to be married and/or have children. You can't say that in front of everyone. That's not cool. They'll think there's something wrong with you. There's even a euphemism for it in the world of online dating: rather than (God forbid!) admit she is looking for a "relationship," a young woman will seek "a partner in crime."

When did that happen? When did it become so bad to say what you really want, to admit the true desires of your heart to your friends, your coworkers, or your lovers? If no one knows what those are, how are you ever going to accomplish them? A person who doesn't care isn't a guy or an alpha or above the fray. They're a sociopath. They're fundamentally inhuman in a very real sense. Today my personal knot has been untied. I've learned so many lessons that now if someone doesn't share my values or goals, I move on. There is always someone else, but there is only one me. If I'm not wanted, or if I'm not getting what I want, then I need to move on.

The question: what *do* I want? When I look back, I can see that at a young age I was always very career focused, and I still am. When people asked me if I wanted to get married and have kids, I'd say that those were eventual goals but that I wasn't ready yet. I never made a big deal about expressing that, yes, I definitely want to be a wife.

Here's another way that feminism has steered women wrong. By encouraging us to think and act like men, by pretending biology doesn't exist, we were never taught about fertility until it was too late. Nobody told me in my twenties that I'd better start thinking about having kids. It was all just, "Go for the gold! Get that job! You don't need a man!" Now you even have parents

gifting their daughters egg-freezing procedures as college grad-
uation gifts.

I know far too many women who had trouble conceiving at an
ancient age like thirty-five. Even if they did manage to get pregnant, many miscarried. I can't begin to imagine the trauma of
one day having a child growing inside you—and then, the next
day, nothing. Then comes the natural fear that it will happen
again. No one told us this would happen, and now we're paying
the price. The emotional cost is insane—to say nothing of the
exorbitant financial cost of fertility treatments.

Mother Nature is not fair. She does not believe in equality, and she is
certainly not a feminist.

The scary part is, there's a big upside to my never having admitted that I wanted to be a mom. If I *had* said that I want a
career *and* I want to be a wife and have children, then I would
look like a failure. The truth is that I haven't achieved half of
that equation. Women are so driven by the need to regard and
present themselves as successful at all things that we're hedging
our bets when it comes to speaking the truth.

Until this book, I'm sure there was a person or two who assumed I didn't want marriage or kids, though I want both. To
them, any success I have in my profession is me compensating
for my complete failure to achieve my "actual" goals. I'm hardly
alone here. I'm in exactly the same position as every currently
childless successful woman. We are regarded as such anomalies
that there must be something else going on, even though many
of us want kids. The fact that so many women act too cool to care
forces everyone else to read between the lines—and they often do
so very, very poorly.

Betty Friedan did an enormous service for women with her
amazing book *The Feminine Mystique.* She talked about the strug-

gle of the confined housewife, and she wanted more for women. Friedan tapped into a frustration that was real in the 1960s, and I thank her for that. But it's undeniable that the natural desires of women's biology have been mocked and jeered in the ensuing years.

In 1992 Hillary Clinton sneered at the idea of being a homemaker, even as she was about to assume the unelected role of first lady. "I suppose I could have stayed home and baked cookies and had teas," she said, "but what I decided to do was to fulfill my profession which I entered before my husband was in public life." That "I suppose" speaks to the idea that being a housewife is something akin to being an astronaut for many such women. Sure, it's theoretically possible, but it's hardly a realistic option.

In my view, being a stay-at-home mom or a housewife is a pretty damn noble goal. It need not be some sort of servant position, either. After all, "the hand that rocks the cradle is the hand that rules the world." The arguments for and against women being full-time moms have been dissected to death in our culture. What hasn't been discussed is the biological aspect to the debate (and I don't mean the "women are genetically born to be mothers" line).

Thanks to feminists like Friedan, women have a great many options for what to choose to do with their lives. The futurist Alvin Toffler discussed the paradox of what he called "overchoice." At a certain point, having more choices makes decision-making *more* difficult, not less. We can decide between ten entrees at a restaurant with ease, but two hundred becomes impossible. It's not only too time-consuming; it's also too psychologically overwhelming.

This is exactly the problem that virtually all young people, men and women alike, have to face with their life goals. We have so many choices that we can't examine every option at length. Obviously I think that the more options and opportunities we have in our country, the better. I'm not Bernie Sanders, who seems to think having twenty types of deodorant is an issue. I'm just pointing out that having choices is complicated, because life is complicated.

There are various techniques we use to winnow down our options. When it comes to career, we can dismiss entire industries if they don't play to our strengths and skill set. If I had to, I'd probably do pretty well as a reporter. But put me in the diplomacy sector and I'd flounder. Figuring out what our strengths and skill sets actually are—as opposed to what we *think* they are—is another challenge that young people have to face. It takes time and it takes experience. It takes failing and it takes learning from our missteps. The dirty little secret, the unfairness inherent in life, is that men and women do not have the same freedom when it comes to this decision-making process—and the reason is biological.

By denigrating motherhood as beneath the modern woman, many girls are postponing examining that as an option until later in life. As my talks with the interns showed, a college-aged girl can tell all her friends that she wants to be, say, a doctor. She will receive universal praise and support. Yet if she said that she regards motherhood as her primary goal, the praise and support will be far less than universal (to say the least). The social pressure is entirely in one direction. It's cool to care about your career, but utterly uncool to care about being a mom.

Postponing marriage and motherhood comes with huge costs—and no one is telling young girls this. It should go without saying that every aspect of pregnancy gets more challenging as women age, from the lower likelihood of conceiving all the way through delivering a happy, healthy baby. It *should* go without saying, but somehow it still needs to be said. Getting pregnant at forty is not the same as getting pregnant at twenty, regardless of career success. Your ovaries and uterus don't care how nice your office is.

Furthermore, the older a woman gets, the smaller the pool of men she has to choose from. Men don't have that problem, for various reasons. I know that women want to tell themselves that it isn't true, and I know there are a lot of movies to the contrary (because everything is so real in Hollywood, of course). But look at the quintessential Hollywood older woman/younger man couple. The Ashton Kutcher and Demi Moore pairing is not the norm. It never was, and almost certainly never will be.

Even that case proves my point. One of the major reasons they broke up is that Kutcher wanted a family and Moore didn't really see that as an option. A woman in her forties telling herself that she is going to be with a twenty-six-year-old is a tad delusional. Sure it happens, but the odds are simply not in her favor. Meanwhile, there are plenty of men in their forties who get together with women in their twenties. That forty-year-old woman could have been a mom and a wife if only she'd let her men—and herself—know that she cared. Women aren't expressing what they really feel and what they really desire. The guys, meanwhile, are getting away with murder.

It's the woman who needs to tell the man to knock the bad stuff out. Eventually the man will *man* up, but it takes a *woman* to demand it. What do you get when you put a bunch of young, immature men together? A frat house, which is the symbol of everything that's disgusting with guys. There's beer cans everywhere, everything smells, and the whole house is a mess. They need a house mother to keep it organized because it's basically one step away from living like Neanderthals.

So when girls start also acting like Seth Rogen—taking bong hits all day every day, sipping whiskey, parading around in boxers, not caring about anything—then the entire culture turns into a frat house. Is that really a good place for young women to be living, in any sense? Is that a good place for men past the age of twenty-one? For kids, for families, for professionals?

These young women aren't fooling me. Of course they care. We're women. We care about everything. We *over*care. The suppressing of emotion is manifesting itself in truly terrible ways for women. They're unhappy because they're not getting what they want—and since they're not asking for what they want, they're never going to get it. Antidepressants and antianxiety prescriptions are on the rise. In one *Glamour* magazine study, women couldn't even define what happiness looked like. They don't even know what it *means* to be happy! "I'm not happy and never will be. Whatever!" How is that healthy or good or positive? It's sick, is what it is.

The cases where female celebrities confess to having female emotions are few and far between. In 2007 *Maxim* voted Sarah Jessica Parker the unsexiest woman alive. It took her six months of ruminating and biting her tongue before she finally decided—and it was obviously a conscious choice—to say something. It was a huge deal that she admitted that her feelings had been hurt. *Of course* they were hurt. To be publicly labeled as the least sexy woman on earth is not only cruel, it's downright humiliating. Yet Parker was expected to pretend that everything was fine. She was rich, successful, and famous, so it shouldn't bother her. Worse, some even said that *because* she was rich, successful, and famous, she didn't have a right to complain.

Obviously few women are as successful as Sarah Jessica Parker.

But as women grow increasingly powerful in every industry, Parker's position—and the criticism of it—can be viewed as a more extreme iteration of a dilemma that *all* women face. Everyone agrees that money, fame, and fortune can't buy happiness. So how are those things supposed to make a person feel comfortable in her own skin? They obviously can't. In fact, the opposite is true. Hollywood celebrities—perhaps the most lauded people in our culture—are needier, more neurotic, and more insecure than the average. They tend to get more elective plastic surgery and to have greater body dysmorphia.

At what point is it acceptable to admit that you care, that it's not just "whatever"? Look at how Jennifer Aniston handled Angelina Jolie snatching Brad Pitt away from her. To publicly have your husband stolen is humiliating and embarrassing. Aniston didn't besmirch Jolie, which took some major self-control. She instead chose to appear above the fray.

Whether on the red carpet or in the workroom, walking around smiling and choosing not to discuss a topic gives off the impression that you're fine, that you've over it. I understand the impetus behind that. You don't want to let the people who wronged you feel like they've scored. But the implication is a pretty dark one. Young people, especially young women, feel as if they can't care about their own problems. After all, those are nowhere near as bad as having your spouse publicly stolen away, right?

Feminists would have women proclaim our traditionally masculine feelings as much as possible while repressing the traditionally feminine ones. And if we *can't* repress them, then we're supposed to lie about having them to begin with. Even a kindergartner knows that being dishonest makes you a bad person, yet this is what feminists actually want. Lie to yourself and to others. After all, a *guy* wouldn't care if his wife was sleeping with Angelina Jolie. He'd want in on the action. Besides, everyone involved in the scenario is a consenting adult who should be able to do what they want. Whatever!

The feminist relationship with marriage is a pretty warped one, in my view. When a bakery refused to bake a cake for a gay couple's wedding, the backlash and outrage was immediate and intense. The vitriol was enormous. But when Jolie broke up a marriage, no one picketed her movies. There were no urgent Facebook petitions against her. Rather than defending a wronged woman, feminists look the other way. That's because, for many on the left, to criticize a woman—*one* woman, virtually any woman—for her behavior is to be a misogynist.

Isn't it amazing that feminists become completely silent when it comes to breaking up a marriage? Suddenly it's "none of our business"? It's downright absurd how arbitrarily the lines are drawn. *Everything* is somehow the business of feminists—until things get too complicated. When reality intrudes on their pat little ideology, they become stymied and self-silenced. That's because, deep down, feminists can't bring themselves to admit that marriage is an admirable goal and something to keep sacred. They may personally want to get married, but to proclaim that getting married can be as important—or even more important—as career success is regarded as the complete negation of all things feminist.

What women are most afraid to admit is the fact that they *are* afraid. We think that we're easily replaceable and so we're not putting value on ourselves. We're giving up everything we have of value for free, and we're not holding the men accountable or asking them for what we want. We're worried that if we ask the guy if he's seeing anyone else (let alone telling him not to!) then he'll tell us he's not into it and move on. Women aren't really okay with the guys sleeping with all these other women, but we're pretending that we are. It's making us crazy—and we're telling no one about it because that looks weak.

I would have no problem with this too-cool-to-care approach if it weren't for one major caveat: *It never works.* Men aren't mind readers. They're not going to know that a woman wants something from them unless and until she asks for it. Men don't even think the same way that women do, so they can't easily deduce what a female is feeling, either. They can make educated guesses based on past experiences, but our thought processes will always be largely alien to them. If you don't expect much from men, then they don't need to deliver very much.

One guy I dated used to disappear for days for work. I remember one time when he went out to California. There were two days when he didn't call (and this is while we were in a serious relationship). We were talking about serious things—except for during those forty-eight hours of silence. He didn't want to be accountable. He thought checking in with me was stupid. He used to mock couples in which one would call the other to let them know their plane had landed safely.

I understood his perspective. I *didn't* need to know that his plane had landed. There is such a thing as checking in so much that you become a pest and oddly annoying. Yet this was the other extreme. It was essentially identical to the silent treatment, that girlfriend move that drives every man crazy. So what did I do? Did I confront him? Nope. I pretended like I didn't care. That was a complete lie, of course, because I *did* care.

I had conditioned a bad behavior. I had an old dog that probably didn't want to learn a new trick—but if he wanted to be with me then he had to. Old dogs can learn if they want to and if you make them. And if they don't want to, it's time to let that dog loose. I was afraid to hold him accountable because he didn't call me for two days, a fear that made no sense since he wasn't going anywhere. I don't even know what I feared other than seeming to care.

Toward the end of our relationship that same type of behavior on his part would repeat itself with increasing frequency. Why wouldn't it? That's what he felt like doing and from all appearances I was fine with it. Sometimes he would go dark for hours at a time; other times it was days. It constantly upset me, and then I had to further stress about biting my tongue. No one has that sort of stamina. It just doesn't work, and the problem only escalates over time.

I'm not a jealous person and I'm not a possessive person. That's not my disposition at all. I spend a lot of time alone and I cherish that time, so I understand and respect when others need time to themselves.

But I understand that women are petrified to start talking about our emotions and/or to start taking some control of a relationship, lest we be labeled crazy or overemotional. We'll be told that we need to calm down and all that wonderful stuff. My point is that the alternative isn't really a better option. There's a delicate balance to be had, and I don't have simple answers to it all. It's a daily struggle, and the struggle is real.

What *isn't* real is the idea that what's good for the goose is good for the gander. Women take things more personally than guys do. If a guy says he doesn't want kids, we hear that he doesn't want kids with *us*. If a guy says he doesn't want to get married, we hear that he doesn't want to get married to *us*. And if a guy says he doesn't want to be committed, we're not supposed to care?

Taylor Swift writes a lot of emotion in her songs. She cares, and she's pretty blunt about her emotions, both good and bad. She lets the guys know that they are never, ever, ever getting back together. She wants to go back to December. There used to be mad love; now there's bad blood. How is Swift treated for being open with her feelings? She gets labeled as the girl who's kind of crazy and can't keep a guy. She's accused of getting women riled up on revenge. Of course that would never happen otherwise, ladies. We *never* want revenge. (I'm laughing out loud as I write this. You should be, too.)

Taylor Swift is being *honest* and authentic. She's so popular because she isn't afraid to be vulnerable, and that takes courage. It's okay to hate a guy you've broken up with! To claim that you don't care about him and don't care about what he's up to now is absurd. *Every* girl cares. Sure, we eventually get to a point where we don't. But in the interim, it's like, "I don't care. I don't care. I don't care that we ended. I'm fine. I'm fine. I'm fine! Who cares?" Then we run home to find out if we can deduce whether he's been at someone's house. We stalk the ex. We stalk his Twitter, we stalk his new girlfriend, we stalk his Instagram and we stalk hers. Guys do it, too, but we do it to a far greater degree.

The way a woman should act after a bad breakup? Like a woman. It's okay to be a little emotional! I was still very sad after past breakups. Yes, I realize *now* that I didn't just dodge a bullet—I dodged a war. But I don't stay buddies after I break up with someone. We don't communicate on the phone and talk about our new relationships. It's too painful for me to speak to my exes. You were with that person every day—and then it's done. It's a death. The mourning period, suffering through loss, is perhaps the one time women should most be allowed to show that we care. Even cats and dogs get depressed when one of their buddies gets put down. But instead young girls are behaving like guys. They try to replace their ex by having all this random sex—and then when *those* guys don't call back, they aren't supposed to care about it. "Everything's great. Whatever." *Really?*

Look, I'm not saying women should go the Britney Spears

route. Maybe I can see using the umbrella handle to smash the window, but shaving your head is a bit much. No one needs to be like Left Eye (RIP), throwing out all his clothes before burning his house down. But those aren't the only alternatives to indifference! I'm not advocating smashing someone's windows or burning anyone's house down or grabbing a golf club a la Elin Nordegren (Tiger Woods's ex). Nor do I advocate being an emotionless robot, whether it's about a guy or something else entirely.

Women nowadays think that they're doing a service to themselves just because they've managed to keep the guy around. They see it as an accomplishment that they're not freaking out; they're not being labeled crazy; they're cool, calm, and under control. I don't see it as an accomplishment so much as I see it as a fraud. The entire relationship is based on deceit, something that is universally understood to be wrong and completely untenable. A woman needs to love herself enough to say that she doesn't want a guy who's going to pee in the corner two feet from her head. It's perfectly cool to consider that a deal breaker.

I had a friend who was afraid to ask her boyfriend if he wanted to get married and have kids. Of course, this is the kind of questioning that scares guys off during the first or second date. Yet she waited five months to bring it up, by which time she obviously had grown attached. Everything was going so wonderfully by then that she wasn't worried about losing him. After all, since they had so much in common, they must have everything in common, right?

"I don't want to get married," he told her explicitly.

"Well," she said, "where do you see us in two years?"

"Uh, still together. But I never want to get married."

She couldn't stop going on about what a jerk he was. I told her she had it exactly backward: she was the jerk in this scenario.

He's a jerk if he tells you from day one that he wants to get married and that he wants kids and that you have all the same goals. Then she would have had every right to get pissed. But he has every right to his own life choices, *especially* if there's no ring on his finger. If a woman doesn't ask and yet she wants to know, then it's *her* fault for not finding out—especially given that the answer in cases like this is often so direct and unambiguous.

Men prefer the direct approach. Waiting months and *then* declaring that you want kids comes off to men like a bait-and-switch. They will say—correctly—that it's unfair to act cool at first and then all of a sudden start to care. Moreover, you just wasted months of your life being completely inauthentic and being silently pissed off that he was upsetting you. Men will not change on their own. Don't let them become time-wasting life stealers.

One of the most common—if not *the* most common—complaints that men have about their significant others is that the woman doesn't know what she wants, that he doesn't know where he stands with her. Women underestimate how simple men are and how receptive they are to being told directly *if* it's presented respectfully, coherently, and objectively. Men like and need boundaries. They respond well to them. I've found that when you do speak up and express what you want in a way that's not screaming, men will almost always be responsive. They prefer a guideline to a huge fight. They prefer to be told to take out the trash than to have their girlfriend walking around mad and withholding sex.

Passive-aggressive snideness is a bad strategy for everyone. As a woman I find it completely repellent when a man is too much of a coward to speak up and instead relies on little digs to get his dissatisfaction across. Men have even less tolerance for that sort of thing—to say nothing of getting the cold shoulder for no apparent reason.

I once got a text from a guy I was dating. "You wanna tell me what I did this time, or should I just keep pretending that I don't notice that you're freezing me out?"

My immediate reaction when challenged is to attack. Too-cool-to-care Andrea wanted to write back, "Keep pretending." Then I remembered how my aggression often backfired in my face in relationships, so I went to Plan B. I wanted to go dark and continue ignoring him, even though he was explicitly asking me what was wrong, with the intention of making it right. After thinking about it for five minutes, I realized that Plan B wouldn't accomplish anything, either. Not only would my silence not change his behavior—and how could it?—it would only cause stress and tension for both of us. It would make me look mean, would not be very mature, and it would not gain me my desired outcome. If I kept it a secret, it couldn't change his behavior. He would certainly do it again. I chose to tell him that he had hurt my feelings, and he *gladly* chose to acknowledge and apologize for what he did. No marginally decent man wants to hurt a girl's feelings—but no one knows what you're thinking but you.

Nine times out of ten the guy doesn't even know what he did wrong. Ninety-nine times out of a hundred a person shouldn't be in a relationship with someone who is indifferent to hurting them anyway—and that includes friendships as well as romantic relationships. In fact, this is a very easy test to see if the guy is someone to be with. If he's too cool to care about causing pain (even accidentally), then there's no point in sticking around with the status quo.

There's a reason why there are traditional guidelines to behavior, but girls aren't asking that guys follow them. We're not asking for what we want. If it takes nine months to have a child, it really shouldn't take nine months to ask for a commitment. It shouldn't take the greater part of a year to admit that you regard marriage and children as more than a passing thought. There's absolutely no question that after several months, the guy has thought about marriage and children as well. No one is being fooled, but everyone is getting hurt.

Unfortunately this is what things have come to in our culture. Young women are encouraged to put themselves out there emotionally, visually, and sexually. They're taught to hold nothing back for themselves—and left to wonder why they are so unhappy. College girls, on average, are having upwards of fourteen partners during one semester, and they're leaving college more depressed and less confident than when they entered. According to one study, female seniors at Boston College left the college with lower self-esteem than when they entered as freshmen. They aren't emotionally mature enough to handle the pressure of feminist directives, which is why they need to internalize the message from a magnet on my refrigerator: *Elegance is refusal.* Resisting is power. Though it's harder to say no than yes, nothing worthwhile is easy. Elegance and the self-respect that comes along with it are well worth it.

Despite decades of feminism, despite wave after wave of activism, women are less comfortable than ever in fighting for their true selves. Meanwhile, men are increasing their power every day. There's no reason for them to treat a person well when that person doesn't seem to care one way or another. There's no reason for them to be committed when they have so many choices. There's no reason for them to keep it in their pants when there's a cornucopia of women willing to cede their sexual power but too afraid to ask for anything in return.

Luckily for the men, there's an app for that.

Chapter 11

The Great American Unraveling

ONE EVENING I was getting mic'ed up for *The O'Reilly Factor*. Before the camera started rolling, Bill and I began to have one of our frequent discussions as to whether the country could get back to traditional values. "We can," he insisted. "If a leader emerges, in the mold of JFK."

"Who would that be?"

"Someone who can captivate the masses and motivate us."

"No way," I said. "We've gone too far. There's no putting the genie back in the bottle."

"Why?"

"Well," I told him, "it's a Tinder nation."

"What's Tinder?" he asked.

What's Tinder indeed.

Imagine a guy sitting on his recliner with a beer in one hand and a remote in the other. Instead of flipping through television channels, the guy is flipping through pictures of women. Eventually he finds one that he likes—or two, or three—and he stops. He presses a few buttons, and then he waits. Within an hour, that same woman in the picture comes to his house, has sex with him, and then leaves. (If he's really hardworking, maybe *he* goes to see *her*.) The woman does this free of charge, with no realistic expectation of future contact and no exchange of money.

Why would any female in her right mind do this? The very premise is absurd. It sounds like a scene from some silly sci-fi comedy. Maybe some android—that I could understand. But a real flesh-and-blood female? Why would she leave her home to meet someone she has only seen a picture of and exchanged a few texts with? The only expectation would be that she'd sleep with the man she's meeting and, very likely, never see him again. Not only is it humiliating and largely exploitive by the man; it's also not going to make her happy.

The scene I'm describing doesn't come from some near-future speculative fiction, nor is it going on in the back alleys and black market of some far-off country. It's happening here and it's happening now—*literally right now*. The people who should be raising a fuss about this sort of behavior—namely, conservatives—aren't even aware that it's going on.

It's all due to a smartphone app called Tinder.

The origins of Tinder lie in an earlier, equally successful app named Grindr. Grindr is an app for gay men. Its purpose is to facilitate random, anonymous sex between two consenting guys. Based on GPS, Grindr tells the user who nearby is looking for sex at that very moment. All it takes is for two men to match in the same area and they can hook up immediately. They can hook up in bathroom stalls, they can hook up in someone's apartment, they can hook up in a car—and they can get away with it.

Of course men would love an app like that—these are the same creatures who are known to think about sex every twenty seconds—and so, naturally, the ingenuity of America's private sector adapted the app for the heterosexual market. Tinder works very similarly to Grindr. It shows the guy one girl's profile picture at a time, women who are within a specified radius. If he wants, he can click on her photo to read her bio. If not, he can simply swipe to the right on his phone if he finds her attractive. If he doesn't, he swipes left. Now his picture will pop up at some point in her Tinder app. If she swipes right as well, Tinder declares a match and the two become free to contact each other.

People are routinely having sex with each other after fewer than ten messages. This is unprecedented. Historically women have been the filters when it comes to intercourse. Men are always on green-light mode when it comes to sex. Women are the yellow lights that slow down the process or we're the red lights that stop it altogether (until we decide that the man is worthy of making us switch the light back to green). We are living, breathing stop lights. Sexually it is the rational, more controlled lady who makes things slow down or grind to a halt if the man isn't acceptable or if she isn't ready. But in Tinder's America, there are no yellow or red lights. It's essentially all green, all the time.

When you really break down the behavior that Tinder invokes, it doesn't really allow for a female to behave in a traditional manner. The most "feminine" traditional choice she can make is to wait for the man to send her the first message. When I talk to my friends who are on Tinder, they actually think that they're being old-fashioned and ladylike if they wait for the guy to make the first move. "Oh, I'm on Tinder but I wait for him to message me! I never message them *first*."

"Well," I say, "what do you do after that?"

"Oh, well, after that we talk. He'll usually set a time and place to meet for drinks and I meet up with him."

Simply because she didn't message him first, somehow this is a woman's last grasp of tradition, and of control.

Wherever I go in New York, whether a store or the subway, I always see people on Tinder. They're on their phone, swiping right and left. People aren't even communicating with each other at bars. This is even happening when real-life women are mere feet away, waiting to be approached. I've seen tables of men together, all of them on their phones, looking to find their next hookup.

What's so shocking to me is that women are willing to go along with this whole scam—and go along with it on terms that are typically reserved for and set by men. Tinder isn't just in major cities, either. It's all over the country, and it is a phenomenon. Just look at the Sochi Olympics. Because Tinder only displays people within a specified radius of the user's location, all the athletes from different countries could connect because they were in the same town. Tinder has gone global—and now Tinder allows you to swipe elsewhere, to set up a hookup in the city you'll be visiting in the near future.

Because most everyone who is single (and many who aren't) are on it, and because it's so easy, people of both genders feel like they're being excluded if they're not swiping with the rest of them. Partly because of this FOMO—"Fear Of Missing Out"— people feel like they're otherwise never going to meet someone. Since just about every guy under the age of thirty-five is on Tinder, avoiding it isn't really an option for throngs of single women, even if they don't like the idea.

People have told me that they join Tinder to find love and relationships, but that's like finding a unicorn. It's the story of the man who leaves his wife in order to marry his mistress, and the two of them live happily ever after—it just doesn't happen. After dozens of interviews, not one woman or man has told me that they started a relationship with someone they met on Tinder, nor did they know a long-term couple who met on Tinder.

To be quite candid I can see the appeal, and why it can be so consuming. The app is very visual. It's based on one thing: looks. And isn't that how we *all* make a first initial judgment, to see if there's that sexual attraction from the get-go? On Tinder, you can actually see the person and are making a decision based on that, rather than some blind date set up by your hairdresser. All it takes to succeed on Tinder is one good picture and you're set.

I don't criticize Tinder for being looks oriented, because that's a reality. Superficiality has been there since the beginning of time. Women and men are visual creatures. One's initial reaction doesn't really come down to a complex formula. A friend could try to set me up with a guy and tell me that he's into politics, tall, athletic, and Greek. But if she showed me his picture and it was the Hunchback of Notre Dame—or even of Thessaly—then we'd have a problem. When you match with someone on Tinder not only do you think they're cute but you know *explicitly* that they found you attractive as well. This empowers men at the expense of women. It also gives both sexes a confidence boost that everyone likes to feel. "Oh, he's hot, and he thinks I'm hot so therefore . . . let's hook up!"

Not too long ago the hunt for the opposite sex had far more intrigue and required much more effort and excitement. Friends would anticipate the evening and spend hours strategizing where they were going to go. A girl would take the time to select a hot outfit and coordinate with her friends. Once a location was chosen, you would meet up with your wingwomen and wingmen and it was on. If the first place sucked, you shifted to a new locale. Sometimes it took a couple of different places to finally find the right crowd. But even in that setting, a woman wasn't guaranteed to meet someone she was going to like.

What *was* guaranteed was that the man had to work for it. Even when a girl surveyed the scene and locked eyes with a potential prospect, it was usually the guy who actually had to seek the girl out and figure out a way to come talk to her. This required, at minimum, getting off his ass, buying a drink, *and* throwing out a semidecent pickup line. It meant actually asking the girl questions about herself. It meant acting like a gentleman so that she—and her friends who were likely watching all eagle-eyed—didn't think he was a complete pervert. It could have meant getting her phone number. Other times, it meant getting her to come home with him (whether they slept together or not). But for most men, all they were working toward was getting that phone number so they could call. The pickup artists even had a term for it: "number closing." Now guys don't need that number. Thanks to Tinder, they get an avenue of contact because some girl on their phone thinks they're cute.

This old-school scenario worked because at their core men are hunters. They're wired to enjoy the conquest and capture the woman. Many men have told me how exciting they find this challenge. After the chase, when they finally see the woman wearing their shirt in the morning, "it's like beholding a conquered flag."

Thanks to Tinder, women everywhere are waving their white flags of surrender. All a guy has to do is swipe instead of work, making the modern male very, very lazy. The toughest thing a man has to do—which isn't tough at all—is to text a stranger who has already affirmed that she finds him attractive in some sense. If she doesn't respond or ceases to text him back he may care . . . for five seconds. Then he moves on because there are hundreds more where the last one came from. Because there was no real and human connection made over, say, drinks or barroom conversation, there is no attachment. This is not exactly romantic risk taking.

In the news business, there's what we call "third-party sourcing," meaning, independent confirmation from someone else.

Not that long ago, the only thing a woman wondered after meeting a guy was how drunk she had been. Was he as cute as she remembered, or had she put on the beer goggles? Women had to go to their friends for independent confirmation. Now there's no way to reassure, since communication *precedes* the first meeting and none of your girlfriends can vouch that he isn't a serial killer.

If a guy really put his mind to it and spent some hours on Tinder, he could match with *dozens* of girls in one night. Why spend evening after evening slathering on the aftershave and engaging in anticipatory man grooming when you only need to get a haircut once, put together the perfect outfit once, and strike a selfie pose—one time. Then you can post that one good picture and use it in perpetuity. There's no effort in looking good. He can literally get sex while sitting on his couch with a Busch pounder and a bucket of chicken.

Take the case of Dick Talens. Yes, that's his real name—I double-checked. (And yes, he insisted I use his full name when discussing him as a case study of how Tinder works.) Dick is highly educated, with a bachelor's degree from Wharton. He's a young entrepreneur, cofounding the fitness social media network Fitocracy before moving on to work for the messaging app Fling. Mashable even did a profile of him after I spoke to him for this book. Here's his actual Tinder profile:

Is this the sort of thing that would be considered normal even five years ago? Not only is his profile not flagged, it's not all that unusual—and it's rewarded. In fact, sometimes it's the girl who takes the first step on Tinder:

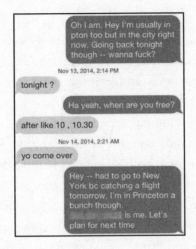

When it comes to texting total strangers, a guy can hide behind his phone. This is one of the reasons why social media has become an intriguing and addicting place—but also a soulless, sick, cowardly, and classless place. A guy can fire off questions like "Wanna bang?" *There's nothing for him to lose.* Guys wouldn't be so forward with their advances if there wasn't a girl somewhere out there who would giggle and say yes, because many already have.

All the social graces, all the protocols and rules—imposed by women—that civilize men and keep them from going against their urges are gone. Women are scared to chastise men that they've matched with. They're afraid of being called crazy, or uncool, or uptight. The boldest thing my friends do when they get a racy Tinder message is to just ghost the guy, disappearing without an explanation. Rarely does a man get ripped to shreds for being too forward.

In the Tinder context, it doesn't make sense for a woman to tell the guy he's acting inappropriately. He'll just tell her that she's a psycho, and then move on to the next one. Women feel that they're badly outgunned because of Tinder; the competition of other women is fierce, so they've got to play it cool even if the guy acts like a pig. They don't want him to walk out the prover-bial door. God forbid! *Not the cute guy from Tinder!* Men are swip-ing their way into sex—and swiping their way out of intimacy and monogamy.

Tinder is destroying our relationships swipe by swipe.

Yet this app is only one side of the equation. In the same way that Tinder is killing discourse in favor of intercourse, the inverse is happening as well. Social media in general and smartphones in particular have brought about a new phenomenon in America: the virtual relationship. People have become unaccustomed to having intimacy and human contact. As a result, we're not even speaking on the telephone. It's too much work to punch in seven digits. There's too much anxiety in trying to call someone—only to risk having them not pick up. Hearing the call go to voicemail is this generation's version of "Sorry, but I already have a boy-friend," "I'm busy," or worse, "Beat it, loser."

We *all* think this way. The other day someone called me and I seized up with fear at the startling, virtually unprecedented sound of a phone ringing. For a minute I almost wanted to duck under the table, terrified that the caller could somehow see me through my phone. And even I was once nervous to dial up men whom I'm dating. I'm afraid that I'm not going to get them on the phone—and then I'll look like the available one because I called them and they didn't pick up. Then what? Is there any big-ger knot than the thorny question as to whether to leave a voice-mail? People no longer even have the courtesy to return a call. I've gotten texts from guys that simply say "Saw that you called." I've had to scream at them to call me back so we wouldn't have to have our conversation over text. Not anymore. In our dating lives today we want immediate return with very little investment and zero risk. In business these deals don't exist—if they do, they're complete shams. The same is true for romance. Never before have we been so connected but so far apart.

So how is this affecting relationships? It's an old cliché but nevertheless true that communication is the basis of a relationship. The way we communicate is changing right before our eyes. Today love has taken a backseat to lust, which is all about texting back and forth. Whether you met at a party or through a friend or on Tinder, you're eventually texting and not actually physically speaking. Men will spend days or even *weeks* texting a woman back and forth like they're in a relationship. The two of them could have been sitting at a dinner, meeting up face-to-face. But men are choosing not to do it.

I call this "Failure to Launch Syndrome," like when I set up my friend Cora with Jake. It turned out he wasn't an outlier, not by a long shot. FTL Syndrome is where two people get themselves into a "relationship" where they don't even know each other. It's causing guys to text "Good night," "Good morning," and "How was your day?" to women they've connected to in some capacity but haven't even *met*. It's giving the guys all the intimacy in a relationship they need (which isn't much) and all the control.

Since I like playing matchmaker, there was another time where I set up a friend of mine with a great guy. He's thirty and comes from a very good family, so I thought he'd have manners and protocol when it came to dating. He saw a picture of her, she saw a picture of him, and I gave him her phone number. Great, my work here is done, right? *Wrong.* Three weeks went by with them being introduced by me via text. Three weeks . . . and he didn't ask her out on a date. At least Jake had the guts to ask Cora to meet his friends.

I wanted to shake him, to tell him to text her and ask her out. Preferably he should *call* her to ask her out, but telling him to call her nowadays would be akin to telling him to climb up her fire escape, or to stand outside her window with a boombox blasting Peter Gabriel. Call her? . . . On the *phone*? Yes, on the phone! That antiquated device where you say things like "Hello, how are you? Would you like to meet up this weekend?" (Adele's song isn't realistic!)

This is only getting worse. Tinder is exacerbating FTL Syndrome. In May 2015 the *New York Times* had an article about the very phenomenon that I'm describing. In an article titled "Swiping Right but Staying Put," they charted the course of two people who met on Tinder. The pair shared laughs and got to know each other over text while they were mere miles apart. They never met face-to-face and when it came time to actually do it, they opted out: "In the end, we had exchanged hundreds of messages for dozens of hours over nearly five straight days. But now that the roads were clear and I was mobile, enabling us to get together in real life, we could be held accountable for our words and affection. That proved to be a burden neither of us could bear." Good grief, people. We're talking about grabbing a coffee, not covering up a murder.

The *Times* also interviewed a guy who had spent hours on Tinder and connected with dozens of girls—but *he never met up with any of them*. When he *finally* decided to meet up with one, to try to convert this relationship-in-absentia into a real-life situation, he found that he couldn't do it. He couldn't handle the anxiety of actually seeing the girl he'd been texting for three weeks. On the one hand, he felt like he knew her because they were texting things like where they grew up and swapping dog pictures. But on the other hand he knew their entire conversation was a façade and a sham. It's easier to text indefinitely than to meet in person and see if there's a *real* connection.

Then there are the guys who are just Tinder teases. *Glamour* magazine featured one of these men in its May 2015 issue.

The subject confirmed that Tinder connections gave him a moral boost but he never sent a woman a text. The reasons? One was "too much expository dialogue," by which he meant the "where are you from" questions that most everyone finds annoying. "Feels like a waste of time" was another. Even men wonder if Tinder can really go anywhere. Another excuse for Tinder FTL? "The flirting is on spec."

"Men are ready to meet women right away," writes the reporter, "but most women need some back-and-forth. I can't blame them. Somewhere between 10 percent and 95 percent of all men are creepy and should be avoided. This means that the Tinder chitchat is an audition, of sorts, to see if men have wit. We're doing it on speculation, hoping that we'll pass the audition and meet in person. No one likes auditions."

Reading news articles and hearing from friends is one thing. It wasn't until I was back on the market that I personally felt just how much the entire game had changed. Guys weren't acting the way they did when I was last single, at twenty-eight years old.

Early on a friend introduced me to a nice guy named Tom. He got my phone number from her and texted me a few days later. I responded and we went back and forth. This continued for days, and still there was no invitation to meet up. My friend would tell me how much he liked me. I could tell from his texts that it was true. Yet, there was no plan to make face-to-face contact! The more I shared this dilemma with friends the more I realized this wasn't an isolated incident with some seriously insecure weirdo. This was an epidemic. It wasn't just the young guys, like I'd suspected. All the men were conducting the same type of effortless "relationship" in absentia. We were all suddenly Scarlett Johansson's character in the movie *Her*, where Joaquin Phoenix's character falls in love with a computer with a sultry voice.

Then there was Nate, whom I met in Miami when I kicked off

the Freedom Tour three weeks after my major breakup. To numb
my pain and get back in the game I grabbed a girlfriend and
headed south for some sun and sangria. I was single and ready to
mingle. Nate and I connected but it wasn't until a few months
later that we started seeing each other—sort of. He lived in Chi-
cago and I was in New York. We continued a long-distance relationship via text message. Nate would text me constantly: "Good
morning, beautiful." He'd text me throughout the day. Even
good night, almost every night. On weekends he'd ask what I
was doing and check in to see if I was home or out. We'd send
pics and occasionally talk on the phone because I would insist
on it. Eventually I had a conversation with Nate—yes, on the
phone—about what a waste of time this was becoming. All these
texts, all these emotions building, but I had nothing to show
for it. We had created a false intimacy that couldn't support the
fantasy. "Nate," I told him, "if I wanted a pen pal I would have
sponsored a child."

Nate had an excuse. He didn't live close to me. I would never
have had that sort of relationship with someone who lived in
New York, but it allowed me to see firsthand exactly what my
friends were all bitching about—and it didn't feel so hot. Thanks
to a larger culture that has conditioned us to commit to nothing, men can't even commit to getting a drink or dinner. In the
famous book *The Rules*, women were told not to accept any date
invitation after Wednesday. If he didn't ask by then, you had to
make him wait till the next week. Now women are lucky if they
get a full twenty-four hours.

Guys are texting women out of the blue with questions like,
"Hey. What are you up to?" If the woman likes the guy she'll
want to respond by saying "nothing" or "not too much" (perhaps a
"leaving the gym"), implying she's free so that he feels comfortable
enough to ask her to get together—that is, if that's what he's look-

ing for. Risk averse, the guy might respond, "Nice. Wanna meet up later?" Everything is so . . . vague. "Maybe." "Cool. I'll text you." He is left with total control, and she is left with questions. When is "later"? Like, late late? Do I still need to make other plans? Does he mean drinks? Will he be alone? *Is this a booty call?*

And there it is: modern-day dating. We're more connected than ever, so why do we feel so disconnected? Only someone who would want distance, not closeness, would use text as a primary communications tool.

With Tinder, every date is essentially a blind date. When you meet in person, you have to show the other party that you're actually who you've been portraying. You have to live up to your perfectly edited photo. This goes for both genders. Maybe you're not as tall, or as thin. "Will she like me?" "Will *he* like *me*? My boobs are pushed up in this picture; they're not as big in person." All that stuff goes through people's heads. In the olden days (like, five years ago), you met someone at the bar and you already knew what they looked like. Now you don't know—and finding out causes anxiety on both sides. So people text and text and text, pen pals instead of partners.

What is increasingly happening as a result is that too much of a relationship is being formed over text. When the two finally meet in person, the conversational reality can't support the fantasy that's been created. No one can live up to those expectations. With texting, a guy can pause to think about how to be witty and funny. He can ask his friend for the perfect response. In person, he's got to reply on the spot. He's got to be charming and engaging in real time. Men are choosing to do the former over the latter—at the cost of actually meeting with women, maintaining this coy back-and-forth flirting that ultimately goes nowhere and wastes time.

Texting is one of the few kernels of control that women haven't ceded to men—and even that is fading fast. I once saw a meme of a girl staring at her phone: "Why won't he text me . . . so I can ignore him?" That's the only way you can play hard to get these days as a woman: waiting to text the guy back. As much as men won't pick up the phone to make a plan, almost every single guy that I dated during the Freedom Tour was upset if I didn't respond fast enough to his texts. Guess what? Texting is a great supplement to a relationship, especially a long-distance relationship or one with two very busy people. But a *supplement* is not a *substitute*.

Before these dating apps like Tinder, Happn, and Hinge, couples were actually spending quality time together. Now a guy who isn't really spending time with any one woman can do pretty much anything that he wants. He's accountable to no one. It used to be a lot harder to juggle other relationships, for both women *and* men. In my twenties I was spending time with that one person. If I wanted to meet someone new it meant going out without him. These days, men can date a woman on a Friday and even if he likes her date others on Saturday and Sunday. He can even double-book. Men are effortlessly conducting a lot of these types of "relationships" with many women at once.

Twenty years ago, not even the most popular person in high school had a hundred friends. Now *everyone* does, because Facebook has completely diluted the meaning of the term. Tinder and similar apps are doing the same thing with regard to "friends with benefits"—a term that should be banned. There is hardly anything beneficial about being someone's sometime slampiece.

While I'm not exactly a Golden Girl, I do remember the days of spending hours on the phone with someone you just met, and how good that felt for both the guy and the girl. The next day you'd recall how you spent a long night talking to a guy before realizing that somehow it had become two a.m. Where did the time go? Guys would blush as they admitted they had found a woman whom they actually loved talking to. People were actually bonding.

Thanks to smartphones, nowadays people are just messaging and messing with one another. Tinder is an app based on *proximity*. People who match live in a one-, two-, or three-mile radius of each other. Ten miles, tops. This is why the lack of real intimacy is so baffling. Instead of physically getting together, one person will message the other one some photos of their dog. Here's what's so nuts: that dog is probably in walking distance, and would love an excuse for some fresh air. What a great reason to make a plan! "Let's go for a walk with Spot and get some coffee after."

Rather than bring the dog to meet the other person, they're telling each other to scope out pics of the very dog on Instagram. "You know, Spot has his own feed. You should check it out." Think how *ridiculous* this smartphone behavior actually is. Who knew a grown person could hide behind something so small? Personally, I think calling it a "smartphone" is the funniest thing I've ever heard. It's the biggest oxymoron of all time. Smartphones enable people to do the dumbest things—and women are dealing with all of them.

Before social media apps, you would have to wait for your girlfriend to bust the guy at the movies with someone else. Girlfriends are alerting other girlfriends when they spot the guy they've been seeing on Tinder. My friend Jane once had three separate friends of hers tell her they connected with the guy she was seeing. Even better: all it takes is for him to like a mystery girl's pics on Instagram. Then a woman can find her page and voila! Pics of the two of them together from the night before. "I *knew* I recognized her shoulder cropped out of one of his pictures from a few nights ago!" *Busted.*

In the last five years, thanks to social media and our natural

need-to-know wiring, females everywhere have developed the research and surveillance skills once reserved for CIA special agents,
high-level assassins, and private investigators. We've learned the
skill of doing background checks on men. We're stalking Instagram, Twitter, and Facebook pages. We're seeing who the guy's
friends are; what girls they're pictured with; where they went to
school; what fraternity they were in; where they worked and who
they worked with. We can basically find out everything on a potential love interest—or have a girlfriend who can.

I can't describe how frustrating it is to cover stories at Fox
News on how our intelligence agencies are unable to gain access
to jihadist websites. I have an idea: let's have the Department of
Homeland Security put a few thousand out-of-work millennials
on the case. Our foreign enemies wouldn't stand a chance. Never
has there existed such a group of women who are skilled at busting dudes and figuring out where they've been in the last twenty-
four hours. The Federal Bureau of Investigation has nothing on
the Female Bureau of Investigation.

All this information can be helpful . . . but I've personally
worked myself up into such a tizzy that many times I have opted
out of meeting a guy after doing too much research on him. "Oh
no. He's wearing a Georgetown Law T-shirt in this Instagram
photo, but he never graduated. What a liar!"

Given this context, the obvious question is, Why the hell are
so many *women* on Tinder? I've had women say, "I didn't want
to do it. It goes against everything I believe in. I really want to
meet a guy the nice, normal way." But most women whom I've
spoken to—especially those who aren't in their twenties—think
it's their only option. They don't see another way to compete in
the dating market.

For busy professional women, there's something to be said for
saving time via Tinder. When I began checking out the app un-

der my friends' accounts, I at first thought it was amazing. Part of me was even a little envious, because there are some really handsome guys on there. Sure, you have to swipe through hundreds of frogs to find the prince, but they're still there waiting to be found. A woman determined to find someone will have a pretty good stable of men to choose from.

My envy increased when one of my friends showed me the pictures of the men that she'd actually matched with. Some had written to her already, a few hadn't contacted her yet, and there were a couple she was waiting to respond to. Now I could definitely see the appeal. For someone like me, who has very little free time, I could match with dozens of men and make contact with very little effort. I wouldn't have to spend lots of time in the public eye. I wouldn't have to stay out late.

But I could and never would be on Tinder as a public figure (even though I know some do it—even some married ones). I'm lucky that I'm the caboose on the cultural train of decency. In my midthirties, the guys I've dated are my age or older and not on Tinder. They missed the movement entirely. But for other women there really isn't any other venue like it to meet guys— let alone ten of them at a clip, even if they are all cads.

This is a real dilemma as you age. Using myself as an example, I can say that my older friends don't set me up with anyone. My girlfriends who are older than me are married and having babies. They don't know a lot of single guys because most of *their* friends are married. They're certainly not going out on the town with me to meet men in the traditional sense. Nor do their husbands really want them going on a literal manhunt with me. When Saturday night approaches I'm putting on my little black dress, and they're putting on their pajamas. "Wanna come over and hang with us and the kids?" No way! Most single friends don't particularly like setting people up, either. It's a lost art, and most people don't want to get involved in case it goes south. People have too much on their plate to worry about anything but their own lives.

Women in their thirties and forties who are single and those who are in that age group and are recently divorced and coming back on the market are feeling pressure to become a part of the social meet market because the twenty-somethings—aka, the competition—are on Tinder. But the twenty-somethings *can* go out and do things the old-fashioned way. They actually have girlfriends to go out with who aren't married, don't have kids, and aren't in serious relationships. They have the option, but they're not doing that. They're on these apps meeting men—which means that the older women have to follow the men there as well.

Being single can feel like being unemployed. You know the situation is temporary, but living it can be extremely stressful for many people. Not having any prospects from potential employers or romantic partners causes many men and women to really freak out. Tinder takes that anxiety away. The seduction of Tinder is that it allows a woman to feel like she's taking steps to meet someone. Now a woman can feel relieved because she matched with a guy. Someone likes her—and look, he messaged her! How much better do out-of-work people feel when someone responds to their resume or calls them in for an interview? It's a sense of hope. There's a feeling like something is happening. It's not total despair because at any moment you could connect with someone.

Sure, a single girl doesn't necessarily have to be on Tinder or any of these other apps. But if she refuses, the math simply isn't in her favor. If a guy isn't in a relationship, then more likely than not he's going to be on it. So even if she manages to meet someone, he's busy at the same time matching with other women on his phone. This is a very common fear for single women and is certainly justified.

Tinder has elevated men and given them unheard-of privileges. The rise of feminism and its power trade took something that was reserved for a very distinct portion of men in the world and delivered it to *everyone*. To have an unlimited number of women's pictures at your fingertips, to have sex with your choice of partners available at the drop of a hat—these were reserved for famous photographers, millionaires, and rock stars. Now they're available to any guy with a beating heart and no open sores—and *one* good photo. *Tinder allows every guy to behave like a rock star.* While I may sound like a paid endorser, I'm not. I'm just giving it straight. And speaking as someone who has actually dated a rock star, let me just say this explicitly: it's not for everyone, especially not for most women.

Females are wired differently than males. We can try to force ourselves to act the same as them, but our *reactions* will inevitably not be the same. The simplest proof? A pair of shows called *The Bachelor* and *The Bachelorette*. With *The Bachelor*, you put fifteen women in a room and they start crying over a man they've only known for sixty seconds. You simply don't see that on *The Bachelorette*—and you never will, for obvious reasons.

The biggest problem with Tinder, as I see it, is this: it's not structured in such a way as to be conducive to leading into real relationships. Despite articles claiming online love is in reach, nobody buys it. Hookup sites masquerading as relationship portals are hardly the next generation of how people find love, but they are certainly contributing to how we find ourselves in a cultural conundrum. "Tinder expedites things" is where the actual benefits end for women. All the app does is open the door to message after message after message. Maybe she'll go out with him, maybe she won't. But even then the questions remain: Is he still on Tinder? Am I not cool enough to actually care and ask him? Has he taken his profile down? How many women is he seeing? If I don't sleep with him tonight, is he going to sleep with someone else? Because he could.

The fact that women have laid down their arms while they laid down their bodies has led to bad consequences. With women feeling disempowered in being able to civilize men, male behavior has coarsened at a rapid pace. This is especially the case when hiding behind a computer, but even that is now falling away. I enjoy social media and like being able to interact with the viewers directly. What I don't like is when the interaction becomes truly inappropriate.

I get tweeted disgusting things every single day. "You give me boners." "I want to hump you." One guy asked if he could "eat my butt with ketchup." (I suppose it's better than hot sauce.) Another wanted to eat pasta off my rear. (Are we talking rigatoni or bowtie?) Other guys like to describe what they're doing while they watch *Outnumbered*. While my friends and I get a kick out of how *nice* some of the male fans are—even that guy on YouTube who makes slow-motion videos of us crossing our legs—social media has made us completely unsocialized and uncivilized.

In just the last couple of years, many of these men haven't even bothered anymore to have a fake profile before tweeting things to me—and to *all* my colleagues—that they would never dare to say in front of *any* female. They know that they're sending their comments to a public person who could easily out them. Every time I read something graphic, I always wonder what would happen if I just retweeted it. I've actually done it once or twice. Rarely, the guys are apologetic. Usually, however, they say nothing. I'm sure some of these guys are so sick that they actually love it.

So how are men talking to women who *don't* have the power that I do? What kind of messages are they sending to women who aren't public figures, women who aren't on television and don't have a lot of social media followers? I've conducted dozens and dozens of interviews with women of all ages who say that the behavior of men has become reprehensible in recent years. I don't mean not picking up the phone to call them, or failing to make a plan for a date. That's rude, but that's not completely outside the bounds of decent, civilized behavior.

I know what guys I've dated have texted me, and there is a level of decorum. They know that there will be repercussions for acting in a completely boorish way. I don't envy women whom men think they can get one over on.

Since men can hide behind their phones, a guy doesn't have to deal with the woman's sense of anger, hurt, or humiliation. And since Tinder matches are a dime a dozen, women aren't calling men out on their behavior. There aren't repercussions, whereas not too long ago it would only take *one* outrageous comment for a man to be labeled a piece of crap and ostracized from his social circle.

A friend of mine recently had a drink, *one drink*, with a guy. She thought they had a good time and she looked forward to seeing him again. Instead she got a text: "Can I come over and suck on your t*ts." He hadn't even bothered to write a question mark! She was horrified . . . but she didn't scold him for it. That comment would have gotten him a slap in the face at a bar. No man would say that to a woman in person. Now he can do it—and if she doesn't like it, he can move on to the next one.

Without the red lights from women, there is only forward momentum. Men now feel emboldened to ask for pictures. I don't mean just shots of the girl, say, making dinner or getting ready to go to work. If she's going to bed he'll ask her to send a photo—and he doesn't mean a cute candid of her brushing her teeth. He wants a picture of her in her nightie, looking like a lingerie ad. I've had this exact type of conversation over and over:

I'm no fun because I wouldn't send a bikini picture? He could have done whatever he wanted with the photo, even if it was "just" showing his friends. Yet he felt comfortable chiding *me* for not being his personal model. We went back and forth and eventually he signed off with the sad-face emoticon :-(. Oh, I'm so sorry you didn't get your belfie! (That's a butt-selfie. Yes, they have a name for that now.) I'm *so* sorry you didn't get a picture of me in my underwear! How are you going to make it through the day? *Will you ever be able to eat pasta again?*

Hey, I have an idea! Why don't you pick up the telephone and make a plan to come see me? Then maybe, just *maybe*, if you don't act like a *total* pig, you will get a second date! Why should I—or any woman—give a man the photo when he hasn't done any-thing to deserve it and when he's in fact done a lot to show that he doesn't respect me? I don't even mean respect in some sort of chaste, maternal sense. I mean respect in the very simple sense of "I respect your preference for not having ass photos of yourself floating around in cyberspace"!

That sense of male entitlement didn't come out of nowhere. Men wouldn't ask for naughty pics if women weren't doing it—and we *are* doing it. We're doing it because that is the norm now, because women are scared to chastise these men. What's the worst a girl can do? Tell him he's a pig? Call him a jerk? Tell him to fuck off and never text him again? Why would he care? He can just go on Tinder and find another girl.

These days if a guy doesn't ask for a picture of a girl's ass on a first date or try to have sex with her, he's basically Prince Charming. The bar for decent behavior is so low, America, that we're tripping over it. There's a big fear of robots gaining artificial intelligence and becoming like us. But it's going in the other direction as well: technology is turning both genders into mindless automatons.

So I ask this: if a woman is going to be a willing party, and she's going to send a guy sexual photos, then why would he bother taking her out for dinner? Guys now can get pretty much *anything* from their phone and their couch. They can have conversations with women who aren't there, and then look at porn and just masturbate—all from the comfort of their own home. I have seen the future, and it doesn't work. It is lazy and it is slovenly. It is *sad*.

So when did this all change? I racked my brain trying to pinpoint a year—and I can't. This didn't happen overnight, and no one thing can fix it, either. But the last decade has clearly been when things changed dramatically. Right after 9/11, our culture had a bit of a Kumbaya moment and it was sincere. For a little bit of time, we all became human beings again. We grew more obsessed with being present, living in the moment, and respecting each other. It felt like we wanted to be better people because we were under attack and so many horrific things were happening.

But all this was just the slow, peaceful creep of a roller-coaster. From our perspective, it was a smooth ride. Then, at some point in the last decade, that roller-coaster went over the first hump and plummeted down the track at a very fast clip. Our culture has been coarsening and deteriorating at a rapid pace, right before our eyes—and the ride ain't over yet.

The World Trade Center attacks weren't the only major current event I can point to with regard to this process. There was also the "mancession" of 2008—culturally speaking, not too long after the events of 9/11. A lot of men lost their jobs in the recession and many others lost their shirts in the stock market. This led to a strain on marriages and to many divorces. A lot of women had to go back to work. Women were getting more power as men lost. Societal protocols were breaking down because women were doing what men were doing. We were earning as much as men, we were going to bars after work, we weren't staying home and raising kids as much because we had jobs. We were at office happy hours and had the same technology that men did. The feminist power trade was already well under way, but the economics certainly expedited it.

Of course, not all of these behavioral shifts can be traced to economics. We like to imagine that every issue has one simple cause, because that implies one simple solution. Human relationships are far more complicated than that. It's really this soup of *everything*. Reality television started a sort of cultural voyeurism and a removal of boundaries—somewhat literally. Now strangers really could see inside a home and watch what was going on behind closed doors. *Big Brother* on CBS and *The Real World* on MTV were huge catalysts for this cultural decay. These shows— and others like them—were fueled by putting people in a house, giving them unlimited amounts of alcohol, and filming it. Television makes previously unacceptable behavior the norm. This can both be a positive or a negative, and clearly in this case we have all lost something.

Finally, there's the effect of technology. Everybody got their hands on a cell phone over the last decade. Cell phones are the one thing that makes us all equal in society. No matter how rich or poor you are, be it an iPhone or an Obamaphone, we've all got one. That Wall Street banker making $20 million and the guy working at Quiznos have the same phone. We all have the same ability to take pictures and selfies. We all have the same apps. For the first time in history, everyone has the power to film themselves and their friends. Technology has equalized everybody.

Congratulations. We're all disintegrating together.

There are a few mainstream outlets—notably the *New York Times*—that do a lot of pieces on Tinder and relationships. But very rarely do any television news outlets talk about Tinder and how relationships are changing at roller-coaster speed. They'll do business stories on Uber, but they won't talk about something that's just as important and has a far bigger impact on our society. In fact, Tinder is like Uber—for sex!

The main media outlets haven't picked up on the cultural decay in America in any real, salient way. They're hyperfocused on the daily news cycle and the latest splashy political scandals. Sure, we may get segments on the breakdown of the American family or why more people are opting out of marriage. But we never really have enough time on television to peel back the layers of the onion and get into the deeper context. It's much harder to report on a creeping long-term problem than on the incidents of the day.

When I bring up Tinder on *Outnumbered*, it's usually just a one-liner that gets a laugh. (No, I don't actually think that conservatives tend to swipe right more often than liberals do.) That's because most of my media colleagues don't even know what Tinder is. They're married and they have kids—there's certainly no reason for them to know what it is on a personal level. Yet the networks are not really following the culture.

It's one thing to talk about people not going to church. It's one thing to talk about why people are being less religious and why America is becoming more secular. But when people are reporting on these types of cultural stories, they aren't really putting their finger on what's going on behind the scenes. Not a lot of people over the age of forty understand Tinder. Even if they know that something called Tinder exists, you kind of have to see it to believe it. I needed to start swiping under the guise of my friends to really get how it connects people.

Yes, Tinder was amazing to me at first. There were this many available and interested men? Great! Yet it's not all great. In the past when you went out with your friends, you'd have funny experiences that led to great memories: "Remember when we met that guy and he wouldn't stop talking about Poison?" Going out to meet people used to be a thing that both women and men did to bond—and now a lot of that is gone. When I criticize Tinder's America, I don't just mean the loss of intimacy between men and women. *Tinder has also removed the intimacy of friendship.*

There are people who recognize that something is going wrong with our culture. Bill O'Reilly senses this as much as anyone. But my biggest debate with Bill is his belief that, if we get the right leader, then somehow we'll magically return to the traditional values that made our country great. My perspective? There's not a chance in hell of that happening.

"We need more principled leaders" is not an answer. The claim is that we wouldn't be having this cultural backslide if only we had appointed certain judges to uphold the law. Judges were being activists who were reversing the religious freedoms in the Constitution, so the right judges would have fixed this. We got away from religion and that's how all "this" (whatever "this" is) happened. It's a very simple narrative: remove God, and now we've all become pagans.

Conservatives speak of this moral breakdown in the abstract and insist on getting back to traditional American values. *What does that mean?* What then do you propose, instead of Miley Cyrus's gyrating MTV Awards performance with Robin Thicke? Because that's how most people are dancing on dancefloors after a few too many Harvey Wallbangers. Ideas, please?

To my ears, "getting back to traditional American values" means let's rewind and return to the 1950s. As much as I don't love what's happening today, that is not only highly unrealistic—it's *petrifying*. As a woman, I don't want to go back there. I don't think *most* women want to go back there. *If I have to choose between feminism and the prefeminist days, I will choose feminism without hesitation.*

Feminism might be better than the past, but we can do better than feminism. Conservatives often attack liberals for their unrealistic ideas. But guess what? There's no DeLorean. There's no time travel. Stop fantasizing about the 1950s. We are here now. Conservatives should be for *conserving*, not *reverting*. What are we *realistically* going to do about our cultural decay?

Abstinence, while very safe, smart, and noble, is a struggle. Monogamy is also a virtue worth pursuing and conserving. The former Arkansas governor Mike Huckabee loves to weigh in on these pop culture debates. But does anyone think Huckabee knows, say, what's going on with Tinder? He's too nice. Would anyone feel comfortable telling him that it's based on Grindr, and opening up that whole can of worms?

Then, when there's someone who's actually getting it right, who's actually being a good role model, who has standards, who's actually being a conservative in some fashion by conserving American values, Huckabee and some on the right go after them. Take the case of Beyoncé. She waited to get married. Then she waited to have a child. She doesn't post naked pictures of

herself. She'll post *sexy* pictures, but compared to everybody else
out there she pretty much covers herself up. She can be provoca-
tive but she's tasteful. She's also got a great relationship with her
husband, Jay-Z. She's not running around on her husband; she's
not cheating; she's a good mother. She's said on multiple fronts
that everything she owes, she owes to her husband.

So what does Mike Huckabee say? "I'm glad to hear someone
preaching family values"? No. He attacks her and says that Jay-Z
is her *pimp*. Never mind that Beyoncé once told Oprah that she's
the woman she is today because she comes home to that man
every night, which is a conservative message. Beyoncé was rich
and famous before Jay-Z. She doesn't need him, but she chooses
to espouse a traditional attitude toward him and their marriage.
Hardly what I would call "a pimp." Yes, she almost certainly
voted for Obama twice. Who cares? And yes, she has pushed
inflammatory anti-cop messages, but those are her politics. Her
personal choices are traditional and should be highlighted by
conservatives, not ridiculed. The bigger issue isn't voting for
Obama, it's the culture. The culture is where we conservatives
miss, because we don't reach high enough. Instead of talking
about cultural decay in *specific, concrete ways* that affect *everyone*,
we look to a medical device tax cut. We're not going to restore
America's promise through tax credits for corporations. We
might win these little battles, but the war is for the culture—
and conservatives lose.

Every. Single. Time.

It is women who civilize men—and it is women, specifically
feminist women, who have uncivilized them. Now the chicks have
come home to roost. The culture is coarsened and it is secular.
It is sex obsessed and self-obsessed. The "folks" (as Bill O'Reilly
likes to call them) are an ever-shrinking piece of America. I'm
glad that millions of people watch Fox News each night—but

there are more than 300 million people in America. Jessica's Law and "the war on Christmas" are *symbolic* fights. These small, anecdotal victories are minor compared with the broader cultural trends over the past fifty years—hell, past *ten* years.

Would *any* current prime-time network comedy have been permitted in 1985? I remember where the only place where you could see a butt cheek on TV was foreign television in Greece or the scrambled Playboy Channel. Now you can say words like *dick* and get away with it. That was *unthinkable* back then. The networks wouldn't even show people sleeping in the same bedroom when I was a child. It was a big deal to have the Huxtables lying in bed and having a conversation. No one can say with a straight face that such massive social change must be an unmitigated good.

Buying a house, going to college, and getting married are all great life accomplishments—but they all bring heavy costs with them, financial and otherwise. *Progress comes at a price.* The left seems to be unable or unwilling to believe that positive changes can also bring with them some serious problems. In the fights that matter, we are losing—and by "we" I don't just mean conservatives. I mean men, and I mean women. I mean all Americans. We are *all* losing *something*.

Hollywood, academia, the media—they've all gone left. Conservatives don't control *any* of them. So if we're going to make a case for saving the culture, we've got to make a compelling case for conserving things that are worth conserving for *everyone*. What are these things that are worth conserving? Here's two big ones: there's intimacy, and then there's respect.

Feminists have tried to politicize every aspect of human relationships. They've succeeded in doing so because the basis of their push was the right one, and that's the aspect of feminism that I am most interested in conserving: *Nobody wants to be treated like crap.* I don't care if you're Republican or Democrat, atheist or

God-fearing. Whatever the case, human beings want love and affection. Nobody wants to feel like a sex object all the time. Sure,
it's probably fine for an hour or so for many people. But *all* the
time? No. People want respect and they want intimacy. No one
wants to be completely alone and sexless for the rest of their life.

Conservatives don't know how to message that. Many on the
right are uncomfortable discussing sexuality at all, so how are they
supposed to criticize misbehavior? In the same way that some feminists expand the definition of rape beyond all meaning, so too do
these conservatives paint all sexual behavior with the same broad,
disapproving brush. Yes, grabbing a girl's breasts and sending her
a naked pic are both bad—but they're not equally bad and they're
not bad in the same way. For many a feminist, any unwelcome
sexual advance is an "assault." To the leftist mind, either everything is allowed or everything must be forbidden. It falls to us
conservatives to define and delineate acceptable behavior.

Against their better judgment, a lot of women are already giving up on the idea of monogamy. Sure, it's not for everyone—
but already the arguments are beginning that it's not for *anyone*.
That's the next shoe to drop in our culture. There are articles
about how to have a nonmonogamous relationship, why polyg-
amy should be normalized, and why open relationships are a
great idea.

Men are not wired to be monogamous. They are wired to
spread their seed and to procreate. It's almost like the dog poop-
ing in the house. The dog will keep it up unless he's conditioned
correctly and told what he's expected to do (or not do). It isn't
an organic thing for a man to say that he doesn't want to have
sex with any other woman for the rest of his life. In *Men and
Marriage*, George Gilder makes the clever observation that the
day that women finally achieve their dream—I finally got him,
I can settle down—is the day that the male's dream dies. His

fantasies of being able to have however many women he wants will be gone.

Women don't take the time to understand that. They don't get it. Women aren't just increasingly afraid to *demand* monogamy—we're becoming afraid to even *ask* for it. We're trying to be too cool and not lose these guys. But men do better *with* boundaries. They *like* them—and they're not in a position to put those in place themselves. Women are better at monogamy, and we're naturally the ones to advocate for it with full sincerity.

Feminists got it wrong because of the power trade. We made a bad deal. While we can't turn back the clock, we can at least set the alarm when something we cherish and hold dear has gone missing, and we want it back. In the quest for what men had, they gave up some of the things that gave women power. Women carry around with them the most powerful weapon everywhere we go. It's the one thing all men want—all straight men, at least—and every woman has one. They're just giving it up. Sex is power, and women control sex.

No one denies the importance of communication. Yet here we are, with ever-increasing *methods* of communication but ever-decreasing attempts at true, honest dialogue. When men are unhappy, they're programmed to bite their tongue and fight back quietly. At the same time, women are complaining—but no one's listening to them. We're just complaining to each other, or playing it cool, and that's not going to untie anything. It's just going to strengthen this disparity between the genders. A knot is supposed to hold two things together, binding them both using each element's strength. Instead people are binding *themselves* up, getting rope burns and constricted in the process. *We're not binding together as human beings, especially long-term.*

It isn't just conservative women who are asking, "Where have all the good men gone?" It's women in general who are realizing that even though a lot has changed—and even though a lot has changed *for the better*—there have been a lot of unintended consequences. Relationships are about deals. We all bring our list of nonnegotiables to the table, and women have had to fight for decades to have their needs heard, respected, and appreciated.

Now the empowered woman knows what she wants in a man and demands as much. He needs to play seven instruments, and speak a foreign language, and be able to cook, and be nice, and love *The Notebook*—but he also needs be a "real man," who steps up, pays the bill, and doesn't have wandering eyes. Fine. A quality woman can afford to be picky. But if the man turns it around and asks what she's going to bring him, the answer is always the same: *nothing*. She's not going to make him a sandwich, she's not going to hand him a beer, and she sure as hell isn't going to have sex with him, because she's too tired. She has too much on her plate, because she's so empowered. There's no longer even a *pretense* to equality here. The two-way street has become one-way, and the old joke about bad female drivers is really coming to fruition in these relationships.

I don't think men are complicated. Here's my approach to the man I love: I give him space; I give him lots of love; I respect him; I give him intimacy all the time. Our culture has disintegrated so heavily, with the genders so divided, that to have a conservative woman advocate such things sounds downright shocking to some people. But this isn't original to me, nor is it new. I don't want to return to the 1950s *Father Knows Best* era. To me, it's Mother who always knows best.

Being pro-marriage isn't enough of a conservative solution, just like it's not enough for a conservative to merely be pro–small business. Some small businesses are horrible—and some marriages are a prison sentence for both parties. Part of what makes a marriage—what makes any romantic relationship—successful is precisely the subject that conservatives are most uncomfortable discussing: sex.

When my mother went to Bible study, the pastor's wife told all the women there the following: "When he comes home, don't have baby throw-up all over you. Brush your hair and put on some lipstick. It takes literally less than a minute. And whenever he wants sex, you give it to him. You always give him attention when he wants it. If you don't, there will be another woman who will." My friend Lisa's grandmother is a missionary in her late nineties, still married to her husband who is close to one hundred years old. She said the same thing: "Always look good, sex on demand."

The deal has never changed: Men have sexual needs, and women have emotional needs. The guy is happy getting sex, and the girl is happy when he listens to her story about her stupid co-worker who stole her idea and didn't give her credit for it. We're not biologically the same. But this should be a source of strength, not a source of antagonism.

Men will have sex at the drop of a hat. Most women need to get into the right mood. Instead of it being a deal breaker, this can be an exciting challenge for the dude. It allows him the thrill of the conquest within the confines of his committed relationship. So rather than "I'm not in the mood, shut up and go away," it can easily become "I'm not in the mood—but would love to be persuaded otherwise."

There's a terrible joke I once heard. Why is a woman smiling so big on her wedding day? Because she knows she gave her last you-know-what. Now imagine if the joke were reversed: Why is a man smiling so big on his wedding day? Because he doesn't have to go down on a woman again. Women would be rioting in the streets. I've even seen a Tinder profile where the girl actually said, "If you don't go down keep walking."

Just because women have all this new power doesn't mean *we* get to oppress now. That was the big gripe with men. As women, we've lost many of the things that made us strong and desirable and uniquely feminine. Why? And for what? We're working harder than ever to be more miserable than ever before.

Kelly Ripa is a great example here. One of the most overworked women on earth is open about how she has wonderful, *frequent* sex with her husband. The reaction from other women is almost palpable: Ripa is making me feel bad about myself. Rather than consider or even try what Ripa is suggesting, it becomes about shouting her down and silencing her. There's no harm in ordering some hot lingerie or pulling a man into the bathroom of a restaurant. Women are digging in their heels when they should be kicking them off.

It quickly becomes a case of "crab in the pot" syndrome. The metaphor refers to a pot of crabs. If the crabs cooperated, they could all easily escape. Instead, as soon as one tries to climb out, the others pull her back in—and so they all end up being stuck. The same thing happens with women. If a Kelly Ripa (let alone an Andrea Tantaros) strays from this mind-set, all the other women quickly go on the attack and make sure she stays the course. God forbid she deviate from the script and find happiness!

Many women believe that equal rights means equal behavior. But being equal doesn't mean that we're the same. Equality in theory became similarity in practice. Feminists turned traditionally male behavior and activity into the standard by which all humans should be judged. In doing so they elevated maleness into an ideal that no man would ever dare advocate for. They wanted to do everything that the men were doing—which included having sex like men. Women have been bamboozled into thinking that if we have sex like men, then we're on their power level. I have equality because I can go out and have sex with ten guys in one weekend. Wow, we're really winning here! Girl power, am I right? Hardly. There is no value in this. In a postmodern world women are allowing themselves to be abused. It's sad.

Feminists aren't happy about what's happening because women are being treated like crap, as worse than prostitutes. They're complaining about it, but it's their fault. They've convinced women that we can behave like men with no strings and somehow it will never come back to affect us. But we're not just shorter men with boobs. We have our own identities and our own needs.

All this is making women deeply unhappy, but feminists have no self-reflection to point out why. Here's why: *Women aren't emotionally equipped to handle it.* That's one thing that feminists never told women, and now we're reaping the mistakes of the misfired power trade. I keep going back to Zosia Mamet and her wondering why the guy she slept with didn't pay for her oatmeal in the morning. Doesn't he owe her that much? Well, *he* doesn't think he does. The one thing that she had—the power—she gave up to be like him. But she's not like him. That's *why* he's attracted to her—*because she's not like him.* He's not gay! He wants the woman.

Greg Gutfeld once joked that women need to unionize, and there's something to be said for that. Women have to step up and we have to start asking for what we really want without fear of repercussion. It sounds very Oprah, but that means getting back to our true selves. Female empowerment means absolutely nothing if we're not really empowered to get what we want. And what do we want? Women don't really want to be having random sex with men who don't call us back. *That's not empowering.*

There are very few women who feel powerful after a one-night stand. I've asked many women how they felt when they ran into a guy they slept with, now on the arm of another female. Any woman who was being honest with herself admitted that she felt like crap. There wasn't some newfound sense of power. They didn't suddenly become inspired to become CEOs. More often than that, they wanted to think of ways to destroy his life. They wanted to call a girlfriend up—after the three hours they spent crying (or during, even). Women really care, and we have to start standing up and advocating for ourselves and what we really want. The men will follow. They always do.

I've seen the progression and challenges by sitting around with women and talking. These early twenty-somethings don't even know what it's like to be on a date. They'll meet in groups of guys and girls, and then it's just a simple exchange of a phone number. Sometimes they'll just end up back at each other's houses, sleep together after a couple of hours—and then all of a sudden they're in a de facto relationship. The man has never courted the woman, he's never had to work for anything, there have never been any rules, no mystery, no guidelines, boundaries, or intimacy. It's all just sort of put out there.

They talk about relationships but no one seems to be really psyched. For a little bit you're excited, but that's it. No one wants to be on Tinder forever. This is why when you ask people if they're happy, they overwhelmingly say no. I think *both* genders are deeply unhappy. They're deeply distrustful of the other sex. They're not respectful of one another. Why should they be?

Maintaining intimacy is very hard. But if both parties don't know how to do it—don't know what it is, what a date is, quality time, talking on the phone, being present—then where are we headed? The apps are only getting more sophisticated. Tinder's competitor Happn is even more like Grindr. Tinder let the user know that there were available people somewhere in their area. It didn't point out that there was someone ready and willing around the corner—literally. That's what Happn does. And now Bumble has taken the last vestige of traditionalism away from women, because on that app it is the females who must initiate the conversation.

We are raising an entire generation of people who don't know how to interact with other human beings. They have no idea what intimacy is. If you don't know what something is and that you've lost it, how do you know to fight for it? How do you know to get it back?

No one, regardless of their politics, can say that diminishing human contact is healthy. Recently there has been a big push from civil rights activists about abolishing or grossly diminishing solitary confinement. They're at their most persuasive when they make the following simple point: Locking up a human being in a tiny cell with no stimulation whatsoever is torture. It's the cruelest punishment, reserved for the worst murderers, and yet we're all desperately going in that direction *as a choice*.

When I speak of intimacy I think of it in all the varied senses of the term. It can be between a couple, or between siblings, or between friends. I think sexual intimacy, and I think emotional intimacy. What it can't be is intimacy without authenticity— and you can't have intimacy without human contact. So what I'm advocating is putting aside the chatter of our neighbors, of the magazines, of the movies, and going back to that internal voice we all have. What is it that you really want? What do you really want to say to this other person? What feelings, what stories, what laughs do you want to share? That doesn't happen over text. Feminists always talk about safe spaces. *Intimacy is a personal safe space between two people.*

When you're with someone, a roll of the eyes or a wink can make a story hilarious. So much of communication is nonverbal that we can interact with people from other cultures who don't share our language—and still crack one another up. Now we've had to invent emojis to demonstrate whether a sentence is meant to be read humorously or angrily.

We're losing intimacy at a daily, constant rate. No one is in the same room with anyone else. No one's even talking on the phone. When I was a teen I could register who wrote a note by glancing at the handwriting. The writing would be infused with someone's personality just from the literal way they crafted each letter. Now I wouldn't be able to identify the handwriting of practically anyone I know (other than people who I grew up with). We're losing ourselves. We're devolving, not evolving.

It is up to conservatives to make the case that there is something worth conserving, something precious that shouldn't just be discarded. I'm talking about values that have been lost within and between the genders, and allowing ourselves to feel and to verbalize what it is we actually want. Gloria Steinem once proclaimed an uplifting answer to the age-old question: Can women have it all? "Women *can* have it all," she insisted. When she was asked about her remarks years later at a conference, she froze. "I never said that. I said women have the right to choose."

On this issue, she's correct. Women can choose. We can choose how to apply our power. We can insist on respect. We can demand monogamy. We can invoke whatever emotion we want. We can choose kindness. We can choose authenticity. We can choose to refuse. We can choose discretion. We can pursue and preserve intimacy in our relationships. But only a conservative can credibly make the case that these things that we've seemingly lost are worth conserving, because only a conservative can truly identify their worth. They are called values with good reason: because they are *valuable*. We must get them back before we slide off a cultural cliff. The beauty is that each and every one of us—women and men—has control over when and how we do this in our own lives. Now that's equality.

These are virtues that are not limited to a gender, race, or political class. They are universal virtues that can make us happier and empower us when pursued and preserved. They are values that will improve the state of our unions, fasten our relationships, bring and bind us closer together—as lovers, as friends, as coworkers, and as a country. They will restore the intangibles that make our souls smile and our lives *better*. And that, my fellow Americans, is something we can all wish for.

With Gratitude

I WANT, FIRST, to thank my mother, Barbara, who taught me that femininity is power; who raised me to be a girl's girl, to always give honor and glory first and foremost to God; and who showed me that it's okay to embrace untying knots with gusto. "Adversity never leaves you where it finds you," you'd say. Ain't that the truth, and I wouldn't change it for the world.

To my precious sister, Thea. Everything they say about sisters is true: there is no bond quite like it. There's nobody else I'd want in my corner when the going gets rough. Or when I need to reclaim a vacuum cleaner, wine opener, and a driftwood mirror without the cops showing up. I'm thanking you first, before Dean, since he got to hold me before you did when Mom brought me home from the hospital because "he's older." You guys are now officially even.

I'm beholden to my brother Dean. Thank you for teaching me about cars, classic rock, how to drive a stick shift, how to stand up to bullies, and for being brutally honest about what men really think. Thanks to you I never made the classic mistake of dropping by a guy's place unannounced. Every girl should be lucky enough to have a big brother who takes the time to teach them these valuable things. But nobody has a better one than me.

To my father, Kosta. I never thought I would be thanking you for being so strict with me growing up. Even though I used to get mad when you'd hang up on boys who used to call the house, I know it was for my own good. I think by now they've all figured out that I didn't move to Greece like you told them. Your legacy is both inspirational and demanding. I will continue to work to honor it and make you proud. I miss you every single day.

I'm eternally grateful to my little brother, Daniel. Your memory reminds me of what's important in life: to stay humble, to be sensitive to those who are different, and to stand up for the weak and the voiceless. You taught me more than I could ever teach you: how to love unconditionally, and that in a world that strives for constant perfection, it's really the flaws that make a person beautiful.

I'd like to thank Roger Ailes for seeing in me, early on, the sociopolitical tour-de-force I've become, and for creating a mega successful platform in Fox News to showcase that passion, much to the dismay of the far left.

Where would I be without my girl squad: Erica Dolgos, Genevieve Hillis, and Ainsley Earhardt. You guys have my back, and I yours.

The stable of friends and allies, who have believed in me professionally and personally, that led me to this moment: Scott and Victoria Park, Joanne Hansen, Kathryn Lehman, Sally Vastola, Greg Crist, Lion Calandra, Bill Smith, Refet Kaplan, and Lynne Jordal-Martin.

Special thanks to Stephanie Barr and Michelle Frazzetta, my book cover glam squad, and my dear friend and stylist, Morgan Lacey, for your fashionable eye that outfitted the cover better than I could have imagined.

Thank you Adam Bellow and the HarperCollins team. Adam, thank you for believing in me and this endeavor.

To all the insanely smart experts who let me pepper them with questions: Phyllis Chesler, Jane Buckingham, Dr. Dendy Engelman, Dr. Allen Rosen, Dr. Keith Ablow, Lux Alptraum, and Eileen Conlan.

I'm eternally thankful to my editor, coach, and buddy, Michael Malice: you restored my faith in people. Even Russians. And you taught me that we don't always "got" ourselves.

Finally, to my Warrior, who showed me that in life there's absolutely no substitute for the love of a good woman or man. I'm forever grateful to you for opening up a part of my heart I never knew existed, for showing me a love that I never knew possible, and for helping me untie the knots.

About the Author

ANDREA TANTAROS is one of the most popular stars on the
Fox News Channel, where she cohosts one of television's
hottest ensemble shows, *Outnumbered*, weekdays at noon, and
serves as a host, political analyst, and columnist for the network.
She has served in senior communications roles on a number of
high-profile political campaigns on Capitol Hill and in corporate
America, and is a former columnist for the New York *Daily News*.
She lives in New York City.